NLT STUDY SERIES

JAMES

Live What You Believe

Norman R. Ericson
Douglas J. Moo

Sean A. Harrison, General Editor

Tyndale House Publishers, Inc.
Carol Stream, Illinois

Visit Tyndale's exciting Web sites at www.nltstudybible.com, www.newlivingtranslation.com, and www.tyndale.com

NLT Study Series: James

Copyright © 2009 by Tyndale House Publishers, Inc. All rights reserved.

Cover photograph copyright © by Helle Bro/iStockphoto. All rights reserved.

The text of James is taken from the *Holy Bible,* New Living Translation, copyright © 1996, 2004, 2007 by Tyndale House Foundation. All rights reserved.

Designed by Timothy R. Botts and Dean Renninger

Edited by Sean A. Harrison

This Bible portion is typeset in the typeface *Lucerna,* designed by Brian Sooy & Co. exclusively for Tyndale House Publishers, Inc. All rights reserved.

TYNDALE, *New Living Translation, NLT,* the New Living Translation logo, and Tyndale's quill logo are registered trademarks of Tyndale House Publishers, Inc.

NLT Study Bible is a trademark of Tyndale House Publishers, Inc.

ISBN 978-1-4143-2197-4 Softcover

Printed in the United States of America

15   14   13   12   11   10   09
7   6   5   4   3   2   1

The purpose of the *NLT Study Series* is to call individuals and groups into serious conversation with God and engagement with his word.

We have designed these studies to provide you and your group with a complete, new Bible study experience. Our aim has been to help you engage seriously with the Bible's content, interacting with it in a meaningful and deeply personal way, not just regurgitating rote answers to fill-in-the-blank questions or producing purely subjective opinions. We also hope to encourage true community study, with the honest sharing of different perspectives and experiences. Most of all, we want to help foster your direct communication with God, encouraging you to tell God what is on your mind and heart. We want to help you understand what God is teaching you and apply it to the realities of personal and community life.

To this end, each study in the *NLT Study Series* includes twelve weeks of individual and group studies focusing on understanding the meaning of the text of Scripture, reflecting on it personally and with others, and responding actively to what God is saying to you through it.

Each volume of the *NLT Study Series* can be used by itself, with no other resources, but you can also use it with your Bible of choice. Each volume of the *NLT Study Series* includes, along with the twelve-week study, one book of the *NLT Study Bible*, with both the text of Scripture and all of the study aids alongside it. The *NLT Study Bible* was designed to open up the world of the Bible and to make the meaning and significance of Scripture clear, so it makes a great personal and small-group study resource.

It is our hope and prayer that these studies will help you and those in your group to understand God's word more clearly, to walk with God more fully, and to grow with one another in relationship with our God.

Open my eyes to see the wonderful truths in your instructions. PSALM 119:18
Come . . . let us walk in the light of the LORD! ISAIAH 2:5

Sean A. Harrison
General Editor

CONTENTS

INTRODUCTION TO THE
James Study

THE LETTER OF JAMES is made up of a series of "mini-sermons." James, probably residing in Jerusalem, was writing to a congregation that had been scattered because of persecution and economic pressures. In their new and difficult surroundings these Christians were dealing with a number of severe problems. Central to this letter is their tendency to try to "have it both ways": They want to be "friends of the world" (4:4) while still being Christian. James's overall purpose is to show that devotion to God must be consistent, undergirding the Christian's way of thinking and lived out in all circumstances. James makes this point in the central passage of the letter (4:4-10) and touches on it in many other places.

This central concern for consistency in our Christian life undergirds the two most famous passages in James. In 1:19-27, he demands that believers must *do* God's word and not just *hear* it. And, in 2:14-26, he insists that faith, if it is genuine, must reveal itself in action. The test of our Christianity is its consistency: We must put into action what we hear and what we profess to believe.

James urges believers to live out this wholehearted commitment to God in many specific ways: in our speech habits (3:1-12), in our community life (3:13–4:3), in our prayer (1:5-8; 5:13-18), in our times of testing (1:2-4, 12-18; 5:7-11). But especially prominent is the theme of rich and poor. Indeed, James has more to say on this matter than any other New Testament book (with the possible exception of the Gospel of Luke). He rebukes his readers for giving preference to the rich (2:1-13) and reminds them that wealth and poverty do not determine our status before God (1:9-11). And, he bluntly condemns selfish and exploitative rich people for their way of life (5:1-6). This theme is of course very timely, striking at the heart of the materialism that so easily creeps into the mindset of those who are well-off.

James's call to a holistic Christianity is needed more than ever. It addresses and rebukes the all-too-common shallowness and superficiality among contemporary believers. Christians who take seriously the message of James will go away from a study of this book with a renewed seriousness about putting into practice the faith that we profess. James teaches, directly and indirectly, a worldview grounded in the Bible and the revelation of God in his Son that sharply contrasts with the prevailing worldview of our culture. James makes it clear, as does the rest of the New Testament, that God is eager in his grace to supply whatever we need to live such a consistent Christian life (see 4:6).

The Letter of James poses four particular challenges to the person trying to understand and apply its message.

FIRST, the letter of James, like other New Testament letters, was written for a particular situation in the life of the early Christian community. James writes to deal with specific problems that his Christian readers are having. James, in other words, is in dialogue with his readers. The problem is that we hear only one end of the dialogue: James's response. What about the other side of the dialogue? What were his readers saying or doing? What specific form did their problems take? We can only guess at the answers on the basis of what James is saying. However, despite this limitation, we must raise these kinds of questions. We must try to discern what the problems were so that we can better appreciate and apply James's answers.

SECOND, James, like other New Testament writers, is using the language of his day. No matter how good a translation is, it can never recapture all the nuances of the language that the New Testament writer is using. A simple word can carry an immense load of cultural baggage, significantly affecting its meaning. The language of being "right" in 2:14-26 is a good case in point. James is tapping into a lively first-century Jewish and Christian debate about "rightness" before God, a debate that has left its traces also in the letters of Paul (especially Romans and Galatians). We cannot go back two millennia and live in James's culture; but using resources such as the *NLT Study Bible* and books about Bible background, we can get an idea about what that culture was like.

THIRD, the distinctive character of James's letter has an apparent lack of continuity in its argument. James moves from topic to topic, and often it is hard to discern a connection. It is important, however, to steer a careful course in this matter. Careful reading of James will often reveal that he has used key words or concepts to connect sections of his letter. However, it is also easy to supply connections that James never intended. Like the Old Testament wisdom books, James may simply be moving from one topic to another without intending any clear connection. The questions throughout this Bible study encourage readers to think about what these connections might be.

FOURTH, James has a distinctive focus on exhortation. The letter of James contains a higher proportion of commands than any other New Testament book. He is consistently in the mode of a preacher calling his people to act in a certain way. James seldom pauses to reassure his readers with comforting theology. Of course, a theology of grace, which James shares with all New Testament believers, is not entirely absent. But its relative paucity means that leaders in studies of James will often do well to bring in the note of grace from the larger teaching of the New Testament.

Douglas J. Moo
Wheaton, Illinois
March 2009

How to Use This Study

THE PRIMARY WAY we recommend using this Bible study guide is for personal daily meditation and study, along with weekly fellowship and discussion.

The introductory session (p. A11) is designed to launch the group study. Group participants need not prepare for this session, but the leader is encouraged to work through it in advance in order to be able to guide the group effectively. The introductory session provides orientation to the book of James, and gives a taste of what the daily and weekly study will be like for the following twelve weeks.

Each week, there are five personal daily studies plus a group session. You can use the daily study guide for your personal daily conversation with God, or you can use it around the table with your family.

You don't need to participate in a weekly group meeting in order to use this study guide. For instance, you can just do the study individually, working through the daily studies and then using the weekly group session as a time of reflection.

Similary, you don't have to use the study on a daily basis in order to benefit from using it in a group setting. You can just do the study with the group each week by reading the passages, thinking about the discussion questions, and participating in the group discussion.

Ultimately, it's between you and God how you use this study. The more you put into it, the more you will get out of it. If you are meeting with a group, we encourage you to decide together what your level of commitment will be, and then encourage each other to stick with it. Then keep up your part of your commitment to the group.

RECOMMENDATIONS FOR DAILY STUDY

Each daily study is designed to be completed within 15 minutes, but optional "Further Study" is usually provided for those who want to go into greater depth.

Start the daily study by reading the passage recommended for each day. Reflect on what it means, and write down your questions and thoughts about it.

You can use the space provided in the book to write thoughts and answers to questions. If you find that you need more space, we recommend purchasing a small blank book with lined paper to use as a Bible study journal. Use the journal to write your answers to the reflection questions, your own thoughts about the passage, what you think God is saying to you, and your prayers to God about what you have studied.

The NLT Study Series is designed to be used with the *NLT Study Bible*. The Book of James from the *NLT Study Bible* is included for your reading and study. You can also use the NLT Study Bible itself, either the print edition or the online version at www.nltstudybible.com. The included section of the *NLT Study Bible* retains its page numbering, so the study guide can be used to refer to either the included section or the *NLT Study Bible* itself.

It can be helpful to highlight or mark the Bible text and study materials where they answer your questions or speak to you in some way. You can:

- underline, circle, or highlight significant words and phrases,
- put brackets around sections of text,
- write keywords in the margin to indicate a topic,
- write page numbers cross-referencing the study guide,
- write dates cross-referencing your journal entries.

Finally, talk with God about what you are learning and how you are responding to it, but also take time to listen to him and hear what he might be saying to you through it. Cultivate your relationship with God day by day.

RECOMMENDATIONS FOR GROUP STUDY

When the group comes together, read the entire passage for the week together, then spend some time letting each person share their own dialogue with God and the Bible that week: insights they've gained, questions they have, and so on.

Then use the discussion questions to stimulate the discussion for that week. You don't have to do all of the questions—you can pick just one.

When the discussion is winding down, spend some time reflecting on what God is saying to you as a group, and how you are going to respond to what God is saying. Spend some time praying together about these things.

Finally, take a look at the passage for the coming week, and make sure everyone understands what they will be doing in preparation for the next meeting of the group.

Orientation to James

SESSION GOALS
- Get oriented to the book of James.
- Discuss what members hope to learn and how they hope to grow in this study.
- Introduce how we are going to be studying together.
- Answer any questions about how to begin.
- Commit ourselves to the Lord and to each other, to participate to the best of our ability.

GETTING ORIENTED TO JAMES
Answer the following questions, either individually, or in discussion together with your group.

What particular issues are you struggling with in your spiritual life?

contentment & peace, instead of anger

How do you think the letter of James might help you in your struggles?

help me restrain my temper with authority figures

How does 2 Tim 3:16-17 apply to our study of James?

James is inspired by God, so it can train me "to be mature and complete"

What factors should we consider when we try to apply a first-century letter like James to our twenty-first-century situation? *the rewards for persevering through temptations hasn't changed, wealth is as corrupting today as it was then*

JAMES INTRODUCTION
Look at the James Introduction, pp. 2110-2112.

Read about the "Setting" of the letter and its "Date and Location of Writing." What might these circumstances tell us about the kinds of issues that the letter was written to address?

Note the quotation in the margin on p. 2111. Then read Jas 4:4. In light of this verse, what does "friendship" with God seem to be, and why is it important?

READING: JAMES 1:1–5:20

Read the entire letter of James aloud. If you're in a group, choose one reader. Read slowly, clearly, and thoughtfully. What questions or observations do you have after reading this letter? Write them down.

STUDY: JAMES 1:1

Who is James? Read the Introduction on "Authorship." Why doesn't he mention his position in the letter? *Jesus' half-brother, so as not to vaunt his position over the others*

How had God prepared James to write this particular letter?

James closely associates "God" and "the Lord Jesus Christ" in his introduction (1:1). What are the implications of this association? *that they are very close, and that they are the same*

Read the study note on 1:1. What is James saying by addressing his readers as the "twelve tribes"? *the twelve tribes were scattered, but God spiritually reunited them*

FURTHER STUDY (Optional)

The letter of James was probably written during the time described in Acts 11:19-21. Read that passage and consider how those circumstances might help us to understand James.

REFLECTION

What is Jas 1:1 saying to you? What might God be saying to you through this passage? *serving God is unconditional, absolute service is how one best serves God*

QUESTIONS

Do you have questions about doing the daily study or preparing for the next meeting?

PRAYER

Take turns praying about this Bible study and the next twelve weeks. You can tell God what your thoughts and questions are, and ask him for his help, strength, and insight. You can thank him for this Bible study and for the Bible itself. You can ask him to speak to you and to the others in the group. The leader, in closing, can also commit this study to God.

God's Purpose in Our Trials: Spiritual Maturity

JAMES
1:2-12

OUTLINE

DAY 1 ◆ James 1:2-4

READING: **JAMES 1:2-12**

Begin with prayer, asking God to give you insight, understanding, and an open heart to listen to and follow his word.

STUDY: **JAMES 1:2-4**

James addresses fellow Christians throughout his letter as "dear brothers and sisters" (1:2, 16, 19; 2:1, 5, 14; 3:1; 4:11; 5:7, 9, 10, 12, 19). What does this say about Christians' relationships with each other?

they are all children of God, so they are all family, and must treat each other as such

Read 1:2. What specific "troubles" were James's readers going through?

religious persecution from the Jews and Romans

In 1:4, James wishes that we would become "perfect" (Greek *teleios*). Look up other instances of this concept: Matt 5:48; 19:21; 1 Cor 13:10; Eph 4:13 ("mature"); Col 1:28; 3:14; 4:12; Heb 6:1 ("mature"); Jas 1:17, 25; 3:2. What, in your own words, seems to be the core meaning of this Greek word?

upright, steadfast, fully grown

The following is the definition of the Greek word *teleios* from the word study dictionary at the back of the *NLT Study Bible*:

> *teleios* (5046), *teleiotēs* (5047): *perfect, complete, mature.* This word describes something that lacks nothing and has come to complete maturity in a particular area. When applied to morality, it means not lacking any moral quality and that each moral quality is fully developed. The noun *teleiotēs* is the state of such completion, perfection, and maturity.

What does James seem to have in mind here when using the word "perfect" (*teleios*)?

absolutely perfect and well-rounded in the faith; strong and fully developed

REFLECTION

What are some troubles that you are experiencing?

family health and peace, stress, anger

What does Jas 1:2-4 have to say to you? What questions does it raise?

perseverance is the method to righteous living, resisting temptation brings safety in the Lord

A14

PRAYER

Talk to God about what you have read, any questions or concerns you might have, and what you think he might be saying to you today. You can write your prayer here if you wish.

DAY 2 ◆ James 1:5

READING: JAMES 1:2-12

Begin with prayer, asking God to give you insight, understanding, and an open heart to listen to and follow his word.

STUDY: JAMES 1:5

Read Jas 1:5 through several times and think well about it.

Why does James encourage us to ask God for wisdom right after 1:2-4?

so that we are able to persevere, because if we try to resist on our own, we may fail without God's wisdom

As the study note on Jas 1:5-8 indicates, "wisdom" is a recurring theme in James (see especially 3:13-18). How is James like other "wisdom" books, such as Proverbs?

gives bits of wisdom in a seemingly unconnected way, gives practical wisdom

Read Prov 2:3-6. What is its message? How does it support what James is saying in Jas 1:5?

If we seek wisdom as fervently as money or treasure, God will give it to us, if we need wisdom, we only need to ask for it

FURTHER STUDY (Optional)

How do we "ask" God for things?

we pray for things that we need, and God chooses to provide, if we ask out of faith

Read Matt 7:7. What does it teach us about how we ask God for things?

we must seek out God to request things, we must ask to receive

What does it mean for our prayer life to realize that God does not "rebuke you for asking" for things?

we will not be rejected for simply asking, but we must make sure we ask unselfishly

A15

REFLECTION

Do you "need wisdom"? Why?

Yes, bodily wisdom, since what wisdom anyone has tends to corrupt, and bodily wisdom only saves

What do you think God is saying to you through your study of Jas 1:5?

if we ask for guidance and wisdom, God will not simply reject it

PRAYER

Talk to God about what you have read, any questions or concerns you might have, and what you think he might be saying to you today. You can write your prayer here if you wish.

DAY 3 ◆ James 1:6-8

READING: JAMES 1:2-12

Begin with prayer, asking God to give you insight, understanding, and an open heart to listen to and follow his word.

STUDY: JAMES 1:6-8

The word translated "generous" in 1:5 could also be translated "single-focused." How does this description of God relate to James's teaching about how we ask God (1:6)?

we must be single - focused on our needs, and we must only trust in God if we can rely on his help

Read 1:6. To whom or to what would James's readers have been tempted to give their loyalty, in place of God?

the leaders of the Jewish community, such as the Pharisees

Read the study note on 1:6. What is the difference between "doubt" and having a "divided loyalty"?

doubt produces insecurity, divided loyalty goes even deeper than insecurity, it alienates oneself from both sides

How does what this note says fit with the theme of "friendship with God" mentioned in the James Introduction?

our faith should only be in God so that we can stay close to him

FURTHER STUDY (Optional)

Read the study note on 1:8. In what ways might you be "double-minded" in your relationship with God? *I trust in my abilities and God, so I should trust in God instead of myself*

REFLECTION

What does Jas 1:6-8 teach you about your prayer life? What are some specific ways that you can change your prayer life to make it more like what James talks about here?
I should pray for God's assistance and guidance in every step I take

What else do you think God is saying to you through your study of Jas 1:6-8?
I shouldn't pray for strength for myself, but for a stronger faith in God

PRAYER

Talk to God about what you have read, any questions or concerns you might have, and what you think he might be saying to you today. You can write your prayer here if you wish.

DAY 4 ◆ James 1:9-11

READING: JAMES 1:2-12

Begin with prayer, asking God to give you insight, understanding, and an open heart to listen to and follow his word.

As you read this short section from James, pay attention to context. What has come before the section? What comes after? How does this context help you understand the section you are reading?

STUDY: JAMES 1:9-11

Read the study note on 1:9-11. Why would poverty and wealth be so important for James's readers that James comes back to it again and again?

Read 1:10 and the study note on 1:10. How does God "humble" rich people?
the rich aspire to greatness, but they will fade in glory if they do not fear God

In the Greek, it is not clear whether "those who are rich" are Christians or not. Are they, or are they not, Christians? *it is implied that they are ungodly as God preserves his servants*

Why does James write about poverty and wealth at this particular place? How does this theme fit into the overall teaching of 1:2-12?

rich people would have divided loyalty with their money and God, but poor people could rely on God more easily

FURTHER STUDY (Optional)

How has God "honored" the poor Christian? In what specific ways would that happen?

poor people find it easier to come to God, and so they are blessed and given glory in heaven

REFLECTION

What does the teaching of this passage suggest about our attitude toward material wealth?

What do you think God is saying to you through your study of Jas 1:9-11?

wealth and fame mean nothing, only God matters

PRAYER

Talk to God about what you have read, any questions or concerns you might have, and what you think he might be saying to you today. You can write your prayer here if you wish.

DAY 5 ◆ James 1:12

READING: JAMES 1:2-12

Begin with prayer, asking God to give you insight, understanding, and an open heart to listen to and follow his word.

STUDY: JAMES 1:12

Why might it seem to be a good idea to study 1:12 along with 1:2-11 rather than with 1:13-15? What specific connections are there between 1:2-4 and 1:12?

it talks about the end goal and reward for perseverance

Read the study note on Jas 1:12. How else could we describe those to whom God has promised "the crown of life"?

Reread the study note on Jas 1:12 and compare Rev 2:10. What is "the crown of life"? *their place in heaven, a promise to live forever after death in peace*

FURTHER STUDY (Optional)

In light of 1:2-11, how do we "patiently endure" testing?

trusting that God will assist me in my trials

REFLECTION

Jas 1:12 suggests that God "blesses" us if we endure testing, and "afterward" we receive the "crown of life." In light of that, what is the blessing that God bestows on us?

What do you think God is saying to you through your study of Jas 1:12?

PRAYER

Talk to God about what you have read, any questions or concerns you might have, and what you think he might be saying to you today. You can write your prayer here if you wish.

GROUP SESSION

READING: JAMES 1:2-12

Read Jas 1:2-12 together as a group.

DISCUSSION

You can use the following questions to guide what you share in the discussion. Give each person at least one opportunity to share with the others.

What did you learn from Jas 1:2-12? What was one thing that stood out to you as you studied this passage? How did Jas 1:2-12 surprise you? Do you have questions about this passage or the study materials that haven't been answered? What does God seem to be saying to you through what you have studied? *one thing was that perseverance produces maturity, so having will power*

TOPICS FOR DISCUSSION

You can choose from among these topics to generate a discussion among the members of your group, or you can write your thoughts about one or more of these topics if you're studying solo.

1. What is the difference between "considering troubles as *an opportunity for* great joy" (cp. 1:2), and "considering troubles *as* joy"? What does the difference have to say about the nature of our God and the world we live in? *they are not inherently good, but can be made good, God wants us to persevere through trials and have joy brow them, trials are everywhere*

2. How does being "double-minded" (see the study note on 1:8) show up in the church today? in your own life? *we are torn between serving God and the evil pleasures of the world, I struggle with these every day*

3. What does 1:9-12 teach about God's plan for prosperity? Is it God's plan to make every Christian wealthy? How can the local church foster the kind of attitude toward poverty and wealth that this passage teaches? *the wealthy will fade and the poor should feel honored, for God protects them, can talk about loving the poor and not loving wealth*

GROUP REFLECTION

What is God saying to us as a group through Jas 1:2-12?

ACTION

What are we going to do, individually or as a group, in response to what God is saying to us? *we should not worry for our needs or prosperity, so I should trust that I will receive all that I require*

PRAYER

How should we pray for each other in response to God's message to us in this passage?

Take turns talking to God about this passage and about what he is saying.

NEXT: JAMES 1:13-18 (Testing and Temptation)

Testing and Temptation

JAMES
1:13-18

OUTLINE

DAY **1** ◆ James 1:13

READING: **JAMES 1:13-18**

Begin with prayer, asking God to give you insight, understanding, and an open heart to listen to and follow his word.

STUDY: **JAMES 1:13**

Read the study note on 1:13. What does James's use of a popular literary style of his day say about the nature of the word of God? *it is adaptive and can move with the times*

Jas 1:12 has connections with 1:2-11. But it also has connections with 1:13-15. What are these connections? *being strong during temptations, and understanding their nature*

Why does James say both that "God is never tempted to do wrong" and that God "never tempts anyone"? *God does not produce temptation, temptation does not come from him*

FURTHER STUDY (Optional)

How does James's claim that God "never tempts anyone" relate to passages such as Gen 22:1 and Judg 2:22? *God tests people's loyalty to him, he does not create impossible tests, and does not create temptation*

The transition from the topic of "testing" to the topic of "temptation" is facilitated by the fact that the same Greek word (*peirasmos*) stands behind both English words. It is not always clear which English word is the best translation. Which do you think is the best choice in Matt 6:13? In 1 Cor 10:13? How do these passages relate to Jas 1:13?

REFLECTION

What are the temptations that affect you most? In what kinds of testing situations do those temptations arise?

A22

What do you think God is saying to you through your study of Jas 1:13?

I can trust that God will help me in the midst of my trials

PRAYER

Talk to God about what you have read, any questions or concerns you might have, and what you think he might be saying to you today. You can write your prayer here if you wish.

DAY 2 ◆ James 1:14

READING: JAMES 1:13-18

Begin with prayer, asking God to give you insight, understanding, and an open heart to listen to and follow his word.

Pay attention to context as you read these verses.

STUDY: JAMES 1:14

How does temptation come from our own "desires" (or "desire": the Greek word here is singular)?

our sinfulness gives us sinful desires, and evil temptations come out of our desires

Read the study note on Jas 1:14. How does James's use of the imagery of trapping and fishing contribute to the idea of the verse?

a person wanders innocently into desire and is dragged irreversibly before he knows it

REFLECTION

If temptation comes from "our own desires," how can you fight against temptation?

What do you think God is saying to you through your study of Jas 1:14?

the sin and temptation sometimes comes from within, instead of without

A23

PRAYER

Talk to God about what you have read, any questions or concerns you might have, and what you think he might be saying to you today. You can write your prayer here if you wish.

DAY 3 ◆ James 1:15

READING: JAMES 1:13-18

Begin with prayer, asking God to give you insight, understanding, and an open heart to listen to and follow his word.

STUDY: JAMES 1:15

The NLT translates the word "sin" (Greek *hamartia*) as "sinful actions." What does this translation suggest about James's meaning here?

sin produces sinful actions

What are the "desires" (or "the desire") that James refers to here?

evil, sinful desires

What is the "death" that sin gives birth to? (Read the study note; and compare Gen 2:17; Rom 5:12; 6:23.) *spiritual death, separation and alienation from God*

What is James's purpose in describing the terrible progression of desires to sin to death? *to show that it is a slippery slope and should be avoided entirely*

FURTHER STUDY (Optional)

Read the following definition for "sinful actions" (Greek *hamartia*): "*hamartia* (0266): *sin*. This noun is a general term for sin, any action or attitude that is contrary to the will of God and the revealed standards of God." Then look up the following passages that use this word: Matt 26:28; Luke 1:77; 3:3; Rom 3:9; 4:7; 5:12; 6:1; 7:8; 8:2; 14:23; 1 Cor 15:56; Eph 2:1; 1 Tim 5:22; Heb 9:26; 12:1; Jas 5:15; 1 Jn 1:9. What is James communicating by using this word in Jas 1:15?

REFLECTION

How does it affect you as a Christian to understand the progression from desires to sin to death? *He smallest evil desire can drag me away and condemn me*

What do you think God is saying to you through your study of Jas 1:15?

PRAYER

Talk to God about what you have read, any questions or concerns you might have, and what you think he might be saying to you today. You can write your prayer here if you wish.

DAY 4 ◆ James 1:16-17

READING: JAMES 1:13-18

Begin with prayer, asking God to give you insight, understanding, and an open heart to listen to and follow his word.

STUDY: JAMES 1:16-17

Does the warning of 1:16 go more with what has come before it (1:13-15)? or with what comes after it (1:17-18)? What is the basis for your answer?

Why does James address his readers again here as "brothers and sisters"? *so they understand that they are family in Jesus*

What similarities are there between the imagery of 1:17 and of 1:6-8? What is James teaching us overall in these passages? *descriptions of nature, man wavers and changes, God does not*

FURTHER STUDY (Optional)

Why would James characterize God here by referring to his creation of planets and stars ("all the lights in the heavens")? *God creates good things and has no darkness in him*

REFLECTION

What are the implications for our prayer life of the claim that "whatever is good and perfect comes down to us from God our Father"?

we should thank God for everything that blesses us

What do you think God is saying to you through your study of Jas 1:16-17?

PRAYER

Talk to God about what you have read, any questions or concerns you might have, and what you think he might be saying to you today. You can write your prayer here if you wish.

DAY 5 ◆ James 1:18

READING: JAMES 1:13-18

Begin with prayer, asking God to give you insight, understanding, and an open heart to listen to and follow his word.

When reading Scripture, always check the margin for cross-references—other biblical texts that might shed light on the passage that you are reading (many of these are listed in the margin of the NLT).

STUDY: JAMES 1:18

Read Ps 136:4-15 (and note that Jas 1:17 cross-references Ps 136:7). How might this Psalm passage explain the transition from Jas 1:17 to 1:18?

God's eternal love prompted his creation of us

What does James's claim that our new birth is something that God "chose" imply about the process of our salvation?

God could have chosen not to save us, but he did because of his eternal love

Read the first part of the study note on 1:18, then read some other New Testament occurrences of the phrase that is here translated "true word": 2 Cor 6:7; Eph 1:13; Col 1:5; 2 Tim 2:15. What do these passages teach us about the process of salvation?

Read the last part of the study note on 1:18. How does the OT language of "firstfruits" help us understand what James is saying about Christians in 1:18?

FURTHER STUDY (Optional)

Does God's plan of redemption include the whole created universe (see, e.g., Rom 8:19-22; Col 1:20)? What are the implications of your answer?

yes, since through man's sin, all the universe fell because of it

REFLECTION

Consider the contrasting processes of birth in 1:15 and 1:18 and reflect on their significance for your standing as a Christian and on your life as a Christian.

What do you think God is saying to you through your study of Jas 1:18?

PRAYER

Talk to God about what you have read, any questions or concerns you might have, and what you think he might be saying to you today. You can write your prayer here if you wish.

GROUP SESSION

READING: JAMES 1:13-18

Read Jas 1:13-18 together as a group.

DISCUSSION

You can use the following questions to guide what you share in the discussion. Give each person at least one opportunity to share with the others.

What did you learn from Jas 1:13-18? What was one thing that stood out to you as you studied this passage? How did Jas 1:13-18 surprise you? Do you have questions about this passage or the study materials that haven't been answered? What does God seem to be saying to you through what you have studied?

TOPICS FOR DISCUSSION

You can choose from among these topics to generate a discussion among the members of your group, or you can write your thoughts about one or more of these topics if you're studying solo.

1. On the basis of Jas 1:13-14, when do we actually sin? When we are tempted? or when we give in to temptation? How does our answer help in fighting temptation?

2. How do we allow sin to grow (1:15)? What can we do to stop its growth?

3. What are the implications of James's calling Christians "firstfruit" (see the study note on 1:18)? What does this language suggest about our role in God's plan for the universe?

GROUP REFLECTION

What is God saying to us as a group through Jas 1:13-18?

ACTION

What are we going to do, individually or as a group, in response to what God is saying to us?

PRAYER

How should we pray for each other in response to God's message to us in this passage?

Take turns talking to God about this passage and about what he is saying.

NEXT: JAMES 1:19-27 (Responding to the Living and Active Word of God)

THREE

Responding to the Living and Active Word of God

JAMES
1:19-27

OUTLINE

Group Session

READING: JAMES 1:19-27

Begin with prayer, asking God to give you insight, understanding, and an open heart to listen to and follow his word.

The paragraphs and headings in our Bibles have been added by editors; they are not part of the original letter of James. As you read James, be careful not to assume that paragraph divisions signal a change to an entirely new topic. There is often a lot of continuity between sections.

STUDY: JAMES 1:19-20

The cross references to Jas 1:19 are Prov 10:19 and 15:1. What light do these texts shed on Jas 1:19? *those who talk alot tend to sin alot, those that control their tongues create brotherhood*

Some interpreters think that being "quick to listen" has as its object God's "true word" (Jas 1:18). What in the context of 1:19 might speak for this view and what speaks against it? *directly mentions both word as an objective, but it talks about righteousness as an objective as well*

How does Jas 1:19-20 contribute to James's argument in this chapter? How do these verses relate to what comes before them and what comes after them? *patience is more desirable to God than boasting about what they could do*

FURTHER STUDY (Optional)

"Righteousness" has several meanings in Scripture. Look up the following passages to get an idea of its range of meaning: Matt 5:20; Luke 18:9; Rom 3:26; 5:17.

What is "the righteousness God desires" that James is talking about in 1:20?

REFLECTION

Is human anger always contrary to God's will? Consider some other passages in Scripture that might help us understand the full biblical teaching on this matter. *not always, as God uses unrighteous anger as well, but not for believers and not good results for the person*

What do you think God is saying to you through your study of Jas 1:19-20?

PRAYER

Talk to God about what you have read, any questions or concerns you might have, and what you think he might be saying to you today. You can write your prayer here if you wish.

DAY 2 ◆ James 1:21

READING: JAMES 1:19-27

Begin with prayer, asking God to give you insight, understanding, and an open heart to listen to and follow his word.

STUDY: JAMES 1:21

How does Jas 1:21 fit in its context? Does it continue 1:19-20 or introduce 1:22?

it carries into 1:22 from 1:19-20 because it talks about using God's word to clear oneself and bring out righteousness

How does the negative command—"get rid of all the filth and evil in your lives"—relate to the positive command—"humbly accept the word"?

removing the filth allows us to accept the word

Why does James refer to "filth" in addition to "evil"?

unclear behavior is part of but not completely defining evil

FURTHER STUDY (Optional)

The study note on Jas 1:21 directs your attention to Jer 31:31-34. Why is this passage helpful in understanding Jas 1:21?

What does "save" appear to mean in this context?

redeem for God, remove our souls from danger

REFLECTION

All the other occurrences of the language "accept the word" in the NT refer to initial salvation (Luke 8:13; Acts 8:14; 11:1; 17:11; 1 Thes 1:6; 2:13). Is that the meaning of the phrase here? Why or why not? And what are the implications? *no, it means to believe and act on it; some Christians receive it but do nothing with it*

What do you think God is saying to you through your study of Jas 1:21?

Talk to God about what you have read, any questions or concerns you might have, and what you think he might be saying to you today. You can write your prayer here if you wish.

DAY 3 ◆ James 1:22-24

READING: JAMES 1:19-27

Begin with prayer, asking God to give you insight, understanding, and an open heart to listen to and follow his word.

STUDY: JAMES 1:22-24

How does the command to do what the word says in Jas 1:22 relate to accepting the word in 1:21? *accepting it requires doing it*

What are people who don't do what the word says "fooling" themselves about?

they think they know it but really don't and forget to follow it

What point is James making with his illustration of the person who looks at his or her face in a mirror (1:23-24)? *if we don't study the word, we will forget it and lose the strength of our faith*

FURTHER STUDY (Optional)

The importance of doing and not just hearing the word of God was widely recognized in James's day. The rabbis taught, "Not the expounding [of the law] is the chief thing, but the doing [of it]." See also Luke 11:28 and Rom 2:13. Why might this have been a problem for James's readers in their particular circumstances?

REFLECTION

What hinders you from doing the word of God? What steps can you take to turn your listening to the word into practical living of the word?

my own courage, if someone needs God and I see it, I should intentionally speak to them and pray for them

What do you think God is saying to you through your study of Jas 1:22-24?

PRAYER

PRAYER

Talk to God about what you have read, any questions or concerns you might have, and what you think he might be saying to you today. You can write your prayer here if you wish.

DAY 4 ◆ James 1:25

READING: JAMES 1:19-27

Begin with prayer, asking God to give you insight, understanding, and an open heart to listen to and follow his word.

STUDY: JAMES 1:25

Why does James use the verb "glancing" in his mirror illustration (1:23) but then change to the verb "look carefully" in his application of the illustration (1:25)?

because the word requires us to study it to learn it, but looking in a mirror does not

Why does James refer to the "law" in 1:25 rather than "word," as in 1:18, 21, 22, 23?

the word of God is God's law as well

Read the study note on Jas 1:25. How does the law "set us free"?

Christ's sacrifice changed the requirements of the law, so now it can save us though Christ

FURTHER STUDY (Optional)

What does the word "law" probably refer to here, given the situation in which James was written (cp. 2:8-13 and 4:11-12)?

REFLECTION

What are specific parts of the law of God that you need to put into practice and so receive God's blessing?

What do you think God is saying to you through your study of Jas 1:25?

PRAYER

Talk to God about what you have read, any questions or concerns you might have, and what you think he might be saying to you today. You can write your prayer here if you wish.

DAY 5 ◆ James 1:26-27

READING: JAMES 1:19-27

Begin with prayer, asking God to give you insight, understanding, and an open heart to listen to and follow his word.

STUDY: JAMES 1:26-27

How does 1:26-27 relate to the teaching of 1:21-25?

talks about practicing true religion and not just talking about it

Why does James include controlling the tongue among the characteristics of true religion? Is there something in the circumstances of James's readers that might explain it? *the tongue influences many other parts of our religion*

Read the study note on 1:26-27. Who are the "helpless members" of your world that you should be caring for? *children who are impressionable and must be taught Christian doctrine*

Why does James add "refusing to let the world corrupt you" to his list of key elements in pure religion? *pure religion resists the world, as it can throw off our beliefs*

FURTHER STUDY (Optional)

In 1:26-27, James mentions three aspects of "pure and genuine religion": controlling the tongue, helping the helpless, and avoiding the corruption of the world. Read through all of James again and summarize how these issues arise throughout.

A34

REFLECTION

James claims that we must avoid the corruption of the world if we are to have a religion that God is pleased with. What are some specific elements of "the world" that are personally affecting you? What can you do to keep them from corrupting you?

The busyness of my schedule draws me away from god, I should deliberately allow time to pray

What do you think God is saying to you through your study of Jas 1:26-27?

PRAYER

Talk to God about what you have read, any questions or concerns you might have, and what you think he might be saying to you today. You can write your prayer here if you wish.

GROUP SESSION

READING: **JAMES 1:19-27**

Read Jas 1:19-27 together as a group.

DISCUSSION

You can use the following questions to guide what you share in the discussion. Give each person at least one opportunity to share with the others.

What did you learn from Jas 1:19-27? What was one thing that stood out to you as you studied this passage? How did Jas 1:19-27 surprise you? Do you have questions about this passage or the study materials that haven't been answered? What does God seem to be saying to you through what you have studied?

the gospel says one can forget what our actions must be an example of the strength of our faith

TOPICS FOR DISCUSSION

You can choose from among these topics to generate a discussion among the members of your group, or you can write your thoughts about one or more of these topics if you're studying solo.

1. List all the references to the word of God and to the law in 1:19-27. What do these descriptions of God's word teach you about the nature of the word of God and our relationship to it?

2. James warns us about fooling ourselves about our relationship with God (1:22, 26). What are some specific ways that Christians today fool themselves about their relationship to God? *people forget to read their Bibles, but they believe they know it sufficiently, relationships based on works*

3. How can we hear God's word in a way that will help us better to do it also?

GROUP REFLECTION

What is God saying to us as a group through Jas 1:19-27?

ACTION

What are we going to do, individually or as a group, in response to what God is saying to us?

PRAYER

How should we pray for each other in response to God's message to us in this passage?

Take turns talking to God about this passage and about what he is saying.

NEXT: JAMES 2:1-13 (The Sin of Favoritism and the "Royal Law")

The Sin of Favoritism and the "Royal Law"

JAMES
2:1-13

OUTLINE

DAY **1** ◆ James 2:1

READING: **JAMES 2:1-7**

Begin with prayer, asking God to give you insight, understanding, and an open heart
to listen to and follow his word.

STUDY: **JAMES 2:1**

James mentions Jesus Christ specifically only twice in the letter (1:1 and 2:1; although see
also 5:7). Why would this be the case? What might explain this, given the situation that
James was addressing?

*the audience is strong in its faith
and belief, but it needed to be taught how
to use it*

Why does James refer to Jesus in such exalted language ("our glorious Lord Jesus Christ")?
How might this reference contribute to James's point (see the study note on 2:1)?

*to distance his blood relation to Christ to
show Christ's superiority*

It is also possible to translate James's description of Jesus as "the Lord Jesus Christ, the
glory." What then would it be saying?

*Christ is glory, and so everything glorious
comes from him*

FURTHER STUDY (Optional)

The Greek word behind "favor some people over others" is *prosōpolēmpsia*. A form of this
word also occurs in Acts 10:34; Rom 2:11; Eph 6:9; Col 3:25; and 1 Pet 1:17. How does
this word help us understand the problem that James is talking about?

*God's judgment is impartial, so we should
not say that anyone's work is superior to
another's*

How does James's concern about favoritism fit into this part of the letter?

REFLECTION

How does our view of God and of Christ affect the way we look at issues in our world?
Does an inadequate understanding of who God is create problems for the way we live?

A38

What do you think God is saying to you through your study of Jas 2:1?

PRAYER

Talk to God about what you have read, any questions or concerns you might have, and what you think he might be saying to you today. You can write your prayer here if you wish.

DAY 2 ◆ James 2:2-4

READING: JAMES 2:1-7

Begin with prayer, asking God to give you insight, understanding, and an open heart to listen to and follow his word.

STUDY: JAMES 2:2-4

Why does James call the church gathering a "meeting," or "synagogue" (see the study note on 2:2)? How might this language reflect the circumstances of the letter?

they were primarily believers, not a church, but brothers in the faith

Why does James choose the contrast of rich and poor to illustrate his point about favoritism (see also 1:9-11 and 5:1-6; and cp. Lev 19:15)?

it is the most identifiable form of prejudice

Is the "rich person" in James's illustration a Christian or not? What difference would it make to his illustration?

yes, it would mean that they knew him personally, but still act differently based on his wealth

FURTHER STUDY (Optional)

As was noted above, the OT also condemns favoritism: see Lev 19:15. Read the context of this Leviticus passage. Why might this verse have been particularly important for James?

it is unjust, a perversion of justice, to show favoritism

REFLECTION

James prohibits favoritism on the basis of the way people in Christian gatherings are dressed. What might this have to say to the way we dress for church and the way we view how others dress for church?

What do you think God is saying to you through your study of Jas 2:2-4?

favoritism goes against God and his natural way of doing things

PRAYER

Talk to God about what you have read, any questions or concerns you might have, and what you think he might be saying to you today. You can write your prayer here if you wish.

DAY 3 ◆ James 2:5-7

READING: JAMES 2:1-7

Begin with prayer, asking God to give you insight, understanding, and an open heart to listen to and follow his word.

STUDY: JAMES 2:5-7

Why does James begin this passage with "Listen to me" (see the study note on 2:5)? What effect should this have on our reading of this passage?

for emphasis, should draw our focus to read it intently

Read the study note on 2:5. Based on the passages mentioned there, how should we understand James's claim that God has "chosen the poor in this world"? Has he chosen all the poor? Has he chosen only the poor? Is this not simply another form of the favoritism that James condemns? Or if not, what is James's meaning?

the poor rely on God more than they rely on themselves, this reliance brings them blessings

Why would rich people be "oppressing" James's readers and "dragging them into court"?

persecution on religious grounds

Biblical writers often begin and end a passage with similar language or ideas. How does James do this in 2:1-7? *speaks of Christs gloriousness and how Christians bear his noble name*

FURTHER STUDY (Optional)

Read the Introduction to James again (pp. 2110-2112). How do the circumstances of the letter illuminate what James says in 2:1-7? Where might we find a similar set of circumstances in our own day?

REFLECTION

What are the implications for you that God has "chosen the poor"?

those who rely on God will receive blessing and future happiness

What do you think God is saying to you through your study of Jas 2:5-7?

PRAYER

Talk to God about what you have read, any questions or concerns you might have, and what you think he might be saying to you today. You can write your prayer here if you wish.

DAY 4 ◆ James 2:8-11

READING: JAMES 2:8-13

Begin with prayer, asking God to give you insight, understanding, and an open heart to listen to and follow his word.

STUDY: JAMES 2:8-11

Read the study note on 2:8. What in the context and in the circumstances James addresses would explain why he calls the law a "royal" law?

the law comes from God, the one true king

What does 2:10 suggest about God's evaluation of our lives and about how we can be saved? *we are all hopeless, unless an act of mercy adjusted the law*

Why has James mentioned the prohibition of "murder" in 2:11? Is there a reason in the context why he might have chosen this particular commandment?

to show two different commandments compared and equalized

FURTHER STUDY (Optional)

Read Lev 19, the passage from which James takes his quotation (Lev 19:18). Is there overlap between James's concerns and Lev 19? What might this overlap suggest about James's letter?

Lev 19:18 is frequently quoted in the NT (see Matt 22:37-40; Luke 10:25-37; Rom 13:8-10; Gal 5:13-14). How does the NT define "neighbor," and how does this affect our understanding of James's teaching here? *the people we meet, especially those in need*

REFLECTION

Who is your neighbor, and what is God calling you to do for that person? *Everyone around me, treat them with respect and protect them*

What do you think God is saying to you through your study of Jas 2:8-11?

PRAYER

Talk to God about what you have read, any questions or concerns you might have, and what you think he might be saying to you today. You can write your prayer here if you wish.

DAY 5 ◆ James 2:12-13

READING: JAMES 2:8-13

Begin with prayer, asking God to give you insight, understanding, and an open heart to listen to and follow his word.

STUDY: JAMES 2:12-13

Biblical authors often use a "bookend" approach as they match the wording or ideas of an opening part of a section or paragraph with the end of that same section or paragraph. Where do you find the other "bookend" that matches 2:12-13? *1:25*

What does James mean by "the law that sets you free" (see also 1:25)? How does it do so? *obedience to Christ frees us from sin*

The margin of the *NLT Study Bible* for 2:13 directs attention to Matt 18:32-35. How does that text illuminate Jas 2:13? And what does it say about the way James has written his letter? *lack of mercy will be repaid with punishment*

FURTHER STUDY (Optional)

How does what James says here relate to the paragraph that follows?

what we do shows our true nature and faith

REFLECTION

James's warning that Christians will be judged by the law stands in some tension with the NT teaching that Christians are saved by their faith alone. How can we integrate these two strands of teaching? *judgment comes from the law, salvation through faith; true faith makes good actions that are not condemned by the law*

What do you think God is saying to you through your study of Jas 2:12-13?

PRAYER

Talk to God about what you have read, any questions or concerns you might have, and what you think he might be saying to you today. You can write your prayer here if you wish.

GROUP SESSION

READING: JAMES 2:1-13

Read Jas 2:1-13 together as a group.

DISCUSSION

You can use the following questions to guide what you share in the discussion. Give each person at least one opportunity to share with the others.

What did you learn from Jas 2:1-13? What was one thing that stood out to you as you studied this passage? How did Jas 2:1-13 surprise you? Do you have questions about this passage or the study materials that haven't been answered? What does God seem to be saying to you through what you have studied?

no mercy for the merciless, favoritism dishonors the poor, since we give their honors to the rich

TOPICS FOR DISCUSSION
You can choose from these topics to generate a discussion among the members of your group, or you can write your thoughts about one or more of these topics if you're study-ing solo.

1. What are some kinds of favoritism that are especially a problem in your community? What kind of response does James prompt you to make?

looks, money, position; treat as equals, since God will show them and me no special treatment

2. How should we understand James's claim that God has "chosen the poor in this world" (2:5)? Has he chosen all the poor? Has he chosen only the poor? And is this not simply another form of the favoritism that James condemns?

3. What does James's emphasis on obeying all the law mean for Christians in practice? In light of passages such as Rom 6:14-15 and 7:1-6, in what sense does the law remain in force for Christians? In what sense does it not?

GROUP REFLECTION
What is God saying to us as a group through Jas 2:1-13?

ACTION
What are we going to do, individually or as a group, in response to what God is saying to us?

PRAYER
How should we pray for each other in response to God's message to us in this passage?

Take turns talking to God about this passage and about what he is saying.

NEXT: **JAMES 2:14-20 (A Living and Active Faith)**

WEEK
FIVE

*A Living and
Active Faith*

JAMES
2:14-20

OUTLINE

Nada?

DAY 1 ◆ James 2:14

READING: JAMES 2:14-20

Begin with prayer, asking God to give you insight, understanding, and an open heart to listen to and follow his word.

STUDY: JAMES 2:14

What connection (or connections) are there between 2:14-20 and the previous parts of the letter? (See the study note on 2:14-26; but also consider other possibilities.)

what someone does will condemn him

Read the study note on Jas 2:14. How is James's message similar to Paul's, and how is it different? *they both talk of true faith; James emphasizes works, Paul emphasizes faith*

Read the passages referred to in the study note on 2:14. Why do you think James does not express here Paul's concern about people "trying to base their relationship with God on what they do"? *his audience wasn't making much effort to do any good works but were*

Why is the particular wording "that kind of faith" especially important in understanding the theology that James is teaching here? *not having a small lazy faith, but having a strong faith that causes action*

FURTHER STUDY (Optional)

What does James's use of the verb "save" here suggest about the focus of this paragraph? Does it have any bearing on the meaning of the Greek word *dikaioō* (translated "shown to be right") in 2:21, 24, 25?

REFLECTION

Does Jas 2:14 imply that it is wrong to claim to have faith unless our lives are perfect? Why or why not? *no, it says to do good deeds and to actively attempt to not sin*

What do you think God is saying to you through your study of Jas 2:14?

PRAYER

Talk to God about what you have read, any questions or concerns you might have, and what you think he might be saying to you today. You can write your prayer here if you wish.

DAY 2 ◆ James 2:15-16

READING: JAMES 2:14-20

Begin with prayer, asking God to give you insight, understanding, and an open heart to listen to and follow his word.

STUDY: JAMES 2:15-16

What is James communicating through this illustration of responding to "a brother or sister who has no food or clothing"? *having faith without practical action does no good*

How does James's illustration fit with emphases of the whole letter?
practical faith

James draws much of his teaching and even wording from the teaching of Jesus (see, for example, the study note on 1:22-23). What passages in the Gospels are you reminded of when you read 2:15-16?

Read the study note on 2:15-16. Should we conclude that it is wrong to pray for people's needs if we cannot meet them ourselves? How can our prayer in such situations be sincere and effective? For example, how should we respond when we encounter homeless people? *no, bring the sight of those who can make a difference to their struggle, give and be generous*

FURTHER STUDY (Optional)

Read 1 Jn 3:17-18, the passage cross-referenced to 2:16 in the margin. How does that text relate to what James says here? And how does it relate to wider themes in James?

What situations in your life are like the one James describes here? What sort of response to those situations would be good?

What do you think God is saying to you through your study of Jas 2:15-16?

PRAYER

Talk to God about what you have read, any questions or concerns you might have, and what you think he might be saying to you today. You can write your prayer here if you wish.

DAY **3** ◆ James 2:17

READING: JAMES 2:14-20

Begin with prayer, asking God to give you insight, understanding, and an open heart to listen to and follow his word.

STUDY: JAMES 2:17

Reflect on James's claim that "faith by itself isn't enough." How does Jas 2:14-16 help to establish this point? *true faith is active, causing positive change through our actions*

Why is faith without "good deeds" considered "dead and useless"? What is James saying about faith? *faith is part of good action, it lives and causes action*

FURTHER STUDY (Optional)

Note some other passages in which the word "dead" is used: Matt 8:22; Luke 15:24; Rom 6:13; Eph 2:1, 5; Col 2:13; Rev 3:1. How do these parallels help us in understanding James's point here?

REFLECTION

Consider your own faith. Is it producing "good deeds"? How can your faith become the kind of faith that consistently produces "good deeds"?

What do you think God is saying to you through your study of Jas 2:17?

PRAYER

Talk to God about what you have read, any questions or concerns you might have, and what you think he might be saying to you today. You can write your prayer here if you wish.

DAY 4 ◆ James 2:18

READING: JAMES 2:14-20

Begin with prayer, asking God to give you insight, understanding, and an open heart to listen to and follow his word.

STUDY: JAMES 2:18

Read the study note on Jas 2:18-19. The "you" in 2:18 is singular because James is using the "diatribe" style (see also the study note on 1:13). How does James's use of this literary device enhance his argument? *everyone is different and has a different gift they can act on*

Read 1 Cor 15:35. How does Paul's wording here help us understand what James is doing in 2:18? *someone ignorant will get a question or say something that throws Christians off*

Consider again the study note on Jas 2:18-19. What is the problem with the objector using 1 Cor 12 to claim a separation between faith and good deeds? *even the enemies of God know he exists and are deliberately evil, so Christians having faith and doing nothing is almost as bad*

FURTHER STUDY (Optional)

The Greek verb behind the NLT "show" is used only one other time in James (3:13, "prove"). How do these passages compare? What light do they shed on each other?

How does James's challenge that we "show" others our faith by our good deeds relate to Jesus' warning in Matt 6:1-2?

What do you think God is saying to you through your study of Jas 2:18?

PRAYER

Talk to God about what you have read, any questions or concerns you might have, and what you think he might be saying to you today. You can write your prayer here if you wish.

DAY 5 ◆ James 2:19-20

READING: JAMES 2:14-20

Begin with prayer, asking God to give you insight, understanding, and an open heart to listen to and follow his word.

STUDY: JAMES 2:19-20

What is the contrast between belief and faith that James is highlighting in these verses?

belief requires no action, faith does

Most of James's readers came from a strong Jewish background. In light of this, why does James choose the belief that "there is one God" as his illustration of the contrast between belief and faith? What does this say about his readers?

They all know there is one God, it is a basic belief, but they are still uncertain about other areas of faith

What seems to be the idea of "faith" that emerges from Jas 2:19?

In Jas 2:20, what exactly is James calling "foolish," and why is it?

lack of good deeds accompanying faith, it is useless for God's purposes

FURTHER STUDY (Optional)

In Jas 2:20, James calls the person he is arguing with (literally) a "foolish person." How does this address fit with Jesus' warning in Matt 5:22?

REFLECTION

What does Jas 2:19 say to you about the nature of your beliefs about God and your "doctrinal" convictions?

What do you think God is saying to you through your study of Jas 2:19-20?

PRAYER

Talk to God about what you have read, any questions or concerns you might have, and what you think he might be saying to you today. You can write your prayer here if you wish.

GROUP SESSION

READING: JAMES 2:14-20

Read Jas 2:14-20 together as a group.

DISCUSSION

You can use the following questions to guide what you share in the discussion. Give each person at least one opportunity to share with the others.

What did you learn from Jas 2:14-20? What was one thing that stood out to you as you studied this passage? How did Jas 2:14-20 surprise you? Do you have questions about this passage or the study materials that haven't been answered? What does God seem to be saying to you through what you have studied?

TOPICS FOR DISCUSSION

You can choose from among these topics to generate a discussion among the members of your group, or you can write your thoughts about one or more of these topics if you're studying solo.

1. Read together the verses listed in the margin next to the note on "Faith and Faithfulness." What do these passages together teach us about the relationship of faith and deeds?

2. What kinds of specific things can we do to avoid the hypocrisy that James talks about in 2:15-16? In general, how can we avoid having "faith" without "good deeds"?

3. How are we to think about James's claim that "faith by itself isn't enough" (2:17) in light of so much emphasis elsewhere in the NT on the unique importance of faith alone?

GROUP REFLECTION

What is God saying to us as a group through Jas 2:14-20?

ACTION

What are we going to do, individually or as a group, in response to what God is saying to us?

PRAYER

How should we pray for each other in response to God's message to us in this passage?

Take turns talking to God about this passage and about what he is saying.

NEXT: JAMES 2:21-26 (Examples of Faith: The Patriarch and the Prostitute)

*Examples of Faith:
The Patriarch and
the Prostitute*

JAMES
2:21-26

OUTLINE

READING: JAMES 2:21-26

Begin with prayer, asking God to give you insight, understanding, and an open heart to listen to and follow his word.

STUDY: JAMES 2:21

Abraham's "offering" of Isaac is a famous OT story. Read Jas 2:21 and the study note on 2:20-26. What is James's purpose in recounting the story of Abraham's "offering" of Isaac? *to show that genuine faith requires real action*

Read the story in Gen 22:1-18. What does this story teach about faith? *people's faith and action, even if it is difficult, will be rewarded far beyond our expectations*

Read another NT reflection on the story in Heb 11:17-19. How does it help us understand James's perspective that "Abraham was shown to be right" in what he did with Isaac? *he had faith that Isaac would live in the end, trusting that God would raise him*

What does the story in Gen 22:1-18, combined with the commentary in Jas 2:21 and Heb 11:17-19, say about Abraham's faith? How was he able to have such strong faith? *he trusted that the best possible outcome would happen, since he trusted completely in God giving him Isaac*

REFLECTION

What is the difference between Abraham's faith and yours? What would need to change for you to be able to follow God the way Abraham did?

What do you think God is saying to you through your study of Jas 2:21?

PRAYER

Talk to God about what you have read, any questions or concerns you might have, and what you think he might be saying to you today. You can write your prayer here if you wish.

READING: JAMES 2:21-26

Begin with prayer, asking God to give you insight, understanding, and an open heart to listen to and follow his word.

STUDY: JAMES 2:22-23

If Abraham's actions "made his faith complete," did Abraham have true faith before his offering of Isaac in Gen 22? *he had true faith, but it wasn't yet shown through action*

Read the study note on Jas 2:22. How were Abraham's faith and actions working together? *he had faith, and demonstrated its strength by acting on it*

In 2:23, James quotes Gen 15:6. Read this verse in its Genesis context and reflect on why James quoted it here. *Abraham wanted an heir and God promised him one, and he immediately believed it, and so built up his faith*

FURTHER STUDY (Optional)

Read the way Paul applies Gen 15:6 in Rom 4:1-8 and Gal 3:6-9. What are the differences between the use of this passage by James and Paul? What do these differences tell us about the relationship of faith and actions? *Paul says that not working is tolerable to avoid sin, but James says that works prove faith, faith is more important than works*

Read the Genesis narrative about Abraham in Gen 12-22. What does his story teach us about the real meaning of faith? *faith is trusting in God guiding our way, but us also taking action and going forward in the way God directs us*

REFLECTION

Are there actions that God is prompting you to do that would make your faith "complete"?

What do you think God is saying to you through your study of Jas 2:22-23?

PRAYER

Talk to God about what you have read, any questions or concerns you might have, and what you think he might be saying to you today. You can write your prayer here if you wish.

DAY 3 ◆ James 2:24

READING: JAMES 2:21-26

Begin with prayer, asking God to give you insight, understanding, and an open heart to listen to and follow his Word.

STUDY: JAMES 2:24

What does the introduction to this verse ("So you see") say about the function of the verse? Note that James switches here to a plural form of "you" (2:22 uses a singular "you"). *it is meant to bring the information we have learned into focus and explain what was there*

Compare Jas 2:24 and Rom 3:28 in several English versions. What are some of the ways that we can reconcile the teaching of these two verses (also consult the study note on Jas 2:24)? *obedience to the law for selfish motives is not true faith, faith is internal and demonstrated unconsciously through good works*

Why is the word "alone" at the end of this verse very important? *having faith is useless if there is no proof of using it*

FURTHER STUDY (Optional)

James again uses the key verb *dikaioō* ("shown to be right"; see also 2:21 and 2:25). Consider how Paul uses this same verb in (among other places) Rom 2:13 and Gal 2:16 ("make us right"/"made right"). How does James's use of the verb compare with Paul's? *James - examples of demonstrated righteousness through actions, Paul - justification through Christ alone*

REFLECTION

If James is right about our being "shown to be right" by "what we do," how much do we need to do to really be shown to be right? How consistent must our doing be? *only enough for us to live righteously, so that we do not surpass the appropriate boundaries and it turns to boasting*

What do you think God is saying to you through your study of Jas 2:24?

PRAYER

Talk to God about what you have read, any questions or concerns you might have, and what you think he might be saying to you today. You can write your prayer here if you wish.

DAY 4 ◆ James 2:25

READING: JAMES 2:21-26

Begin with prayer, asking God to give you insight, understanding, and an open heart to listen to and follow his word.

STUDY: JAMES 2:25

Compare Jas 2:25 with 2:21. What do these verses have in common?

demonstrating the faith and actions of a godly person

Read the story of Rahab in Josh 2:1-24, in addition to the study note on Jas 2:25. How does this OT story serve to illustrate James's point?

she professed her faith in God and proved it by hiding and helping the spies

REFLECTION

Rahab's faith was astonishing, leading her boldly to step out from her culture and embrace a "new God." How might God be calling you to step out from your culture in faithfulness to your God?

What do you think God is saying to you through your study of Jas 2:25?

PRAYER

Talk to God about what you have read, any questions or concerns you might have, and what you think he might be saying to you today. You can write your prayer here if you wish.

DAY 5 ◆ James 2:26

READING: JAMES 2:21-26

Begin with prayer, asking God to give you insight, understanding, and an open heart to listen to and follow his word.

Scripture often uses figures of speech and illustrations in communicating its message to us. James is especially fond of them. Think carefully about what each one might be saying to us, but don't make the mistake of reading too much into them.

STUDY: JAMES 2:26

What other parts of the Jas 2:14-26 passage say something similar to what we find in 2:26?

2:16, 2:20, 2:24

It would seem to make more sense for James to compare the body to good works (concrete) and breath to faith (insubstantial). Why does he reverse the comparison? What point is he making?

He assumes that the audience has faith, and that the works should not be obvious to motivate selfishness

How does James's general point in 2:26 fit with the two examples he has cited (Abraham and Rahab)?

Abraham and Rahab proved they had real faith, because faith is dead without works to support it

REFLECTION

What do we say to Christians who claim to have faith but do not seem to be living very faithful Christian lives? What would James suggest as a way to help them become more consistent in their faithfulness to Christ?

What do you think God is saying to you through your study of Jas 2:26?

PRAYER

Talk to God about what you have read, any questions or concerns you might have, and what you think he might be saying to you today. You can write your prayer here if you wish.

GROUP SESSION

READING: JAMES 2:21-26

Read Jas 2:21-26 together as a group.

DISCUSSION

You can use the following questions to guide what you share in the discussion. Give each person at least one opportunity to share with the others.

What did you learn from Jas 2:21-26? What was one thing that stood out to you as you studied this passage? How did Jas 2:21-26 surprise you? Do you have questions about this passage or the study materials that haven't been answered? What does God seem to be saying to you through what you have studied?

TOPICS FOR DISCUSSION

You can choose from among these topics to generate a discussion among the members of your group, or you can write your thoughts about one or more of these topics if you're studying solo.

1. The problem of reconciling James's and Paul's teaching about faith and works is a famous one in the history of theology. How does the NLT translation (see Jas 2:21, 24, 25) help us to solve this tension? Are there other ways of solving this tension?

2. What is the remedy that James suggests for Christians who are not living a faithful Christian life? What would be the ramifications of this remedy in your life and your community?

GROUP REFLECTION

What is God saying to us as a group through Jas 2:21-26?

ACTION

What are we going to do, individually or as a group, in response to what God is saying to us?

PRAYER

How should we pray for each other in response to God's message to us in this passage?

Take turns talking to God about this passage and about what he is saying.

NEXT: JAMES 3:1-12 (Glorifying God in Our Speech)

WEEK

SEVEN

Glorifying God in Our Speech

JAMES
3:1-12

OUTLINE

DAY 1 . . . James 3:1-2

DAY 2 . . . James 3:3-5

DAY 3 . . . James 3:6-8

DAY 4 . . . James 3:9-10

DAY 5 . . . James 3:11-12

Group Session

READING: **JAMES 3:1-12**

Begin with prayer, asking God to give you insight, understanding, and an open heart to listen to and follow his word.

STUDY: **JAMES 3:1-2**

Read the study note on 3:1. The culture of James's day focused on honor and shame. While becoming a member of the early Christian community may have brought shame (Christianity was viewed as a cult, or worse), teachers were highly honored in the church. What danger for the church might James have been addressing in that situation?

the fact that what teachers said could make or break the early church

Why does James suggest that teachers will be "judged more strictly"? (Consider the teaching of Matt 18:6 and Luke 12:48.) *they are responsible for the doctrine their congregation heard, so in a way they were responsible for their faith as well*

The same Greek word that in Jas 3:2 is translated "make . . . mistakes" is translated "has broken" in 2:10. What does this suggest about the kind of "mistakes" James had in view?

sins, transgressions, every sin both big and small

FURTHER STUDY (Optional)

James uses the word "perfect" (Greek *teleios*) to describe complete self-control. The NLT Study Bible word study dictionary states, "This word describes something that lacks nothing and has come to complete maturity in a particular area. When applied to morality, it means not lacking any moral quality and that each moral quality is fully developed. The noun *teleiotēs* is the state of such completion, perfection, and maturity." Also read Matt 5:48; 1 Cor 13:10; Eph 4:13; Col 3:14; Heb 6:1; Jas 1:4; 3:2.

What kind of perfection does James have in mind? Is it attainable? What is James's point with reference to the role of the teacher? *complete mastery overcoming our sinful nature, no,*

James draws from the OT and from the teaching of Jesus. He also uses Jewish teaching from his own day. For instance, what he says in 3:2 sounds very much like a passage in the intertestamental book *Sirach*: "A person may make a slip without intending it. Who has never sinned with his tongue?" (19:16, RSV). What would James accomplish by referring to popular Jewish teaching of this kind?

What are the implications of God's judging some people "more strictly"? Does God have a sliding scale of evaluation? Is this fair?

What do you think God is saying to you through your study of Jas 3:1-2?

PRAYER

Talk to God about what you have read, any questions or concerns you might have, and what you think he might be saying to you today. You can write your prayer here if you wish.

DAY 2 ◆ James 3:3-5

READING: JAMES 3:1-12

Begin with prayer, asking God to give you insight, understanding, and an open heart to listen to and follow his word.

STUDY: JAMES 3:3-5

James uses three illustrations in 3:3-5. What do these illustrations have in common?

small objects influence great creatures and objects

Why does James stress that the rudder makes the ship turn "wherever the pilot chooses to go"? What application to the human use of the tongue might James have in view?

"Makes grand speeches" in Jas 3:5 could also be translated "boasts of great things." What grand things can the tongue speak about? (As you answer, consider the cross-reference in the margin of 3:6: Matt 12:36-37.) *triumphs, bad things you are secretly proud of, things you are proud of that put people down*

Why has the NLT put the second half of Jas 3:5 into a separate paragraph? *it goes into talking about fire and its relationship to the tongue*

REFLECTION

Reflect on the power of words. What are some specific occasions on which your own words have had great effect?

What do you think God is saying to you through your study of Jas 3:3-5?

Talk to God about what you have read, any questions or concerns you might have, and what you think he might be saying to you today. You can write your prayer here if you wish.

DAY 3 ◆ James 3:6-8

READING: JAMES 3:1-12

Begin with prayer, asking God to give you insight, understanding, and an open heart to listen to and follow his word.

Many NT passages have a formal "quotation" from the OT, set off with quotation marks in our Bibles. But more often the NT alludes to the OT, using language from particular passages to make a certain point. As you read this passage, be alert to those allusions. Use the marginal references to assist you.

STUDY: JAMES 3:6-8

How do James's other uses of the word "world" (1:8, 27; 2:5; 4:4, 8) help us understand his use of the word in 3:6? *evil, corruptive influences of the present society*

Read the study notes on 3:6. James claims that the tongue is "set on fire by hell itself" and that "no one can tame the tongue." Does James intend these claims to be understood as always true? *no, as he is demonstrating in his letter*

In first-century Jerusalem, *Gehenna* referred to the valley of Hinnom south of the city, which was used to burn garbage, and many of James's readers would have understood this connection. What do you think James meant when he said that the tongue is set on fire by *Gehenna*? *It burns brightly, filled with things that aren't pure and only pollutes oneself*

Read the study note on 3:8, then read Gen 3:1-7. What was the "deadly poison" of the tongue in that context? What does James mean by this description here? *lies, the sin that doomed mankind came from the lies of a poisonous serpent*

James is probably depending to some extent on the teaching of Jesus. Read Matt 15:1-20. What are the parallels with Jas 3:6-8?

REFLECTION

In what sense is the tongue "a whole world of wickedness . . . restless and evil, full of deadly poison"? How can James make such strong claims? Does his emphasis on the tongue correspond with the way you usually think of your own speech habits?

What do you think God is saying to you through your study of Jas 3:6-8?

PRAYER

Talk to God about what you have read, any questions or concerns you might have, and what you think he might be saying to you today. You can write your prayer here if you wish.

DAY 4 ◆ James 3:9-10

READING: JAMES 3:1-12

Begin with prayer, asking God to give you insight, understanding, and an open heart to listen to and follow his word.

STUDY: JAMES 3:9-10

In Jas 3:9, James describes the duality of the tongue. What point in the preceding verses does this duality illustrate? *the tongue can tear people down while it tries to bless people as well, they contradict each other and make the speaker a hypocrite*

Read the study note on Jas 3:9. Why does James mention here that human beings are "made in the image of God"? *they resemble God, and so do those around them, so they should treat each other as such*

Why is it unnatural and improper ("not right") for "blessing and cursing" to "come pouring out of the same mouth"? *they contradict, are irrational, and should not happen in anyone*

REFLECTION

James contrasts our praise of God and our cursing of other human beings as a clear example of the duality of the tongue. What other ways do we use our tongues both for good and for evil?

What do you think God is saying to you through your study of Jas 3:9-10?

PRAYER

Talk to God about what you have read, any questions or concerns you might have, and what you think he might be saying to you today. You can write your prayer here if you wish.

DAY 5 ◆ James 3:11-12

READING: JAMES 3:1-12

Begin with prayer, asking God to give you insight, understanding, and an open heart to listen to and follow his word.

STUDY: JAMES 3:11-12

James shows his love of illustration again by using four separate, brief illustrations in 3:11-12. Why has James chosen to use these particular illustrations? What points about the tongue do these four illustrations make? *they were common facts of life the audience knew of, if you were in fact righteous, you would not be able to do the evil things we do*

How do passages such as Ps 64:3 and Prov 5:4 shed light on James's use of the word "bitter" in Jas 3:11? *painful, evil, hurtful, hateful*

REFLECTION

What resources does James suggest will enable you to avoid the terrible duality in your speech habits that he condemns in these verses?

What do you think God is saying to you through your study of Jas 3:11-12?

PRAYER
Talk to God about what you have read, any questions or concerns you might have, and what you think he might be saying to you today. You can write your prayer here if you wish.

GROUP SESSION

READING: JAMES 3:1-12
Read Jas 3:1-12 together as a group.

DISCUSSION
You can use the following questions to guide what you share in the discussion. Give each person at least one opportunity to share with the others.

What did you learn from Jas 3:1-12? What was one thing that stood out to you as you studied this passage? How did Jas 3:1-12 surprise you? Do you have questions about this passage or the study materials that haven't been answered? What does God seem to be saying to you through what you have studied?

TOPICS FOR DISCUSSION

You can choose from among these topics to generate a discussion among the members of your group, or you can write your thoughts about one or more of these topics if you're studying solo.

1. The OT wisdom book Proverbs contains a lot of teaching about speech, and James undoubtedly has this teaching in mind as he writes this paragraph. Reflect on some of these passages from Proverbs as a way of getting a better idea about the specific forms of speech that James might be talking about: Prov 10:8, 18, 21; 11:9; 12:6, 18-19, 25; 13:3; 15:1, 23; 16:28; 17:27-28; 18:2, 7, 13; 25:11; 27:2, 5-6; 29:2, 11, 20.

2. James warns us that the tongue is "restless" (3:8) and is horrified that "out of the same mouth" flow both blessing and cursing (3:10; see 3:11-12). How do these comments fit with the larger themes of the letter of James. (Take a few minutes, if you like, to skim through the letter once more.)

3. James suggests that our speech habits are an indicator of our spiritual health. What do your speech habits reveal about the state of your soul? What can you do about it?

GROUP REFLECTION

What is God saying to us as a group through Jas 3:1-12?

ACTION

What are we going to do, individually or as a group, in response to what God is saying to us?

PRAYER

How should we pray for each other in response to God's message to us in this passage?

Take turns talking to God about this passage and about what he is saying.

NEXT: **JAMES 3:13–4:3 (The Peace That Comes from Godly Wisdom)**

The Peace That Comes from Godly Wisdom

JAMES
3:13–4:3

OUTLINE

READING: JAMES 3:13–4:3

Begin with prayer, asking God to give you insight, understanding, and an open heart to listen to and follow his word.

STUDY: JAMES 3:13

The letter of James is similar to the OT wisdom books (like Proverbs and Ecclesiastes) in that it often moves from topic to topic without direct connection between them. But often there is an indirect connection. Can you see a connection between James's warnings about the tongue (3:1-12) and this new section (3:13–4:3)?

those who are wise control their tongues and say good things instead of evil

Considering the previous verses (3:11-12), who might James have in mind when he speaks of a person who thinks he or she is "wise"? *Jewish leaders and experts of the law*

Why does James mention "the humility that comes from wisdom" as a way in which we are to do good works? What does this say about our good works?

our wisdom should be humble, not self-serving or arrogant

FURTHER STUDY (Optional)

Read the study note on 3:13 and the passages that it refers to. How does wisdom provide an antidote to the problems that James is addressing?

REFLECTION

Do you know other people whom you consider "wise"? How do they reveal that wisdom? How might you become more like them?

What do you think God is saying to you through your study of Jas 3:13?

PRAYER

Talk to God about what you have read, any questions or concerns you might have, and what you think he might be saying to you today. You can write your prayer here if you wish.

DAY 2 ◆ James 3:14-16

READING: JAMES 3:13–4:3

Begin with prayer, asking God to give you insight, understanding, and an open heart to listen to and follow his word.

STUDY: JAMES 3:14-16

Aristotle uses the Greek word translated "selfish ambition" (Jas 3:14) to characterize the partisan politicians of his day. How does this kind of "selfish ambition" manifest itself in communities, like the church? *jealousy of people's faith, desire for recognition, high value in eyes of others*

How do we "cover up the truth" when we boast (3:14)? What are we boasting about? How does this harm the cause of Christ? *we make ourselves greater than other people, people turn away when christians boast or are arrogant*

How do jealousy and selfish ambition lead to "disorder and evil of every kind" (3:16)? *pride is the root of other sins, so having jealousy produces unrest and sin*

FURTHER STUDY (Optional)

What might James have in mind when he warns about "evil of every kind"? How can worldly wisdom bring so many different kinds of evil?

Read 1 Cor 3 (note that the margin of Jas 3:16 refers us to 1 Cor 3:3). What does this passage add to your understanding of "worldly" wisdom and the quarrels it causes?

REFLECTION

Why are the worldly wisdom of jealousy and selfish ambition incompatible with God's wisdom? What are the remedies for these vices?

What do you think God is saying to you through your study of Jas 3:14-16?

PRAYER

Talk to God about what you have read, any questions or concerns you might have, and what you think he might be saying to you today. You can write your prayer here if you wish.

DAY 3 ◆ James 3:17-18

READING: JAMES 3:13–4:3

Begin with prayer, asking God to give you insight, understanding, and an open heart to listen to and follow his word.

STUDY: JAMES 3:17-18

What virtue does James especially highlight in 3:17-18? What in the circumstances of his readers might lead him to focus on this virtue? *peacefulness, early persecution*

Read the passages listed in the margin of 3:18 (Prov 11:18; Isa 32:17; Matt 5:9; Phil 1:11). How does what James say in 3:18 compare with these other passages, especially Jesus' teaching in Matt 5? *if we invest in peaceful relationships and righteousness, we will receive a sure reward from God*

What is the "harvest of righteousness" that peacemakers reap (Jas 3:18)? What else does it include in addition to what is mentioned in the study note? *peace, justice, friendship*

FURTHER STUDY (Optional)

The marginal note on Jas 3:16 refers to Gal 5:20-21. What parallels do you see between that passage and Jas 3:15-17? What are the differences?

REFLECTION

To what extent are you a peacemaker? How can you plant more seeds of peace in relationship with others?

What do you think God is saying to you through your study of Jas 3:17-18?

PRAYER

Talk to God about what you have read, any questions or concerns you might have, and what you think he might be saying to you today. You can write your prayer here if you wish.

DAY 4 ◆ James 4:1

READING: JAMES 3:13–4:3

Begin with prayer, asking God to give you insight, understanding, and an open heart to listen to and follow his word.

Remember that chapter divisions and verse numbers are not part of the original letter of James. Be ready to see continuity between chapters.

STUDY: JAMES 4:1

How does the theme of Jas 4:1-3 relate to what James discusses in 3:13-18?

jealousy and showing wisdom

Where are the "quarrels and fights" that James refers to occurring? What in the circumstances of the readers might have led to these fights? *conflict*
between church members

In light of the connection with Jas 3:13-18, what is the antidote to these "quarrels and fights"? *the wisdom from God*

REFLECTION

How do the evil desires that are "at war" within us lead to quarrels with other people? Can you identify situations in which you have seen this in your own life?

What do you think God is saying to you through your study of Jas 4:1?

PRAYER

Talk to God about what you have read, any questions or concerns you might have, and what you think he might be saying to you today. You can write your prayer here if you wish.

DAY 5 ◆ James 4:2-3

READING: JAMES 3:13–4:3

Begin with prayer, asking God to give you insight, understanding, and an open heart to listen to and follow his word.

STUDY: JAMES 4:2-3

Does the claim that people "want what [they] don't have" resonate with you or sound familiar? How are you personally influenced or affected by the "acquisitive urge" that is so common? *yes, I see the way richer people live and feel a little jealous*

Read the study note on Jas 4:2. The "Zealots" were Jews so "zealous" for God that they felt justified in using violent means to secure Israel's independence. How might the fights and quarrels that James was addressing in the Christian community have been similar to the violence of the Zealots? *they could have conflicts among them about the old and new laws*

What does James see as the underlying cause of these conflicts? And what solution to the problem is implied in his assessment? *the evil desires within people, asking God and receiving wisdom*

What does James probably refer to with the language of "fight and wage war" (see Jas 4:2 and consider the marginal reference to 1 Jn 3:15). *the Zealots killing and fighting*

A74

FURTHER STUDY (Optional)

You can learn a lot about different interpretations of a passage of Scripture by comparing different translations. Read several other translations of Jas 4:2-3 (in English or other languages that you know). What differences of interpretation do you see?

REFLECTION

In light of 1 Jn 3:15, what is the significance of James's warnings in this passage for us in our Christian lives?

What do you think God is saying to you through your study of Jas 4:2-3?

PRAYER

Talk to God about what you have read, any questions or concerns you might have, and what you think he might be saying to you today. You can write your prayer here if you wish.

GROUP SESSION

READING: JAMES 3:13–4:3

Read Jas 3:13–4:3 together as a group.

DISCUSSION

You can use the following questions to guide what you share in the discussion. Give each person at least one opportunity to share with the others.

What did you learn from Jas 3:13–4:3? What was one thing that stood out to you as you studied this passage? How did Jas 3:13–4:3 surprise you? Do you have questions about this passage or the study materials that haven't been answered? What does God seem to be saying to you through what you have studied?

TOPICS FOR DISCUSSION

You can choose from among these topics to generate a discussion among the members of your group, or you can write your thoughts about one or more of these topics if you're studying solo.

1. How can the people of God engage in discussion and decision making without the quarrels that James condemns in this passage? Are all quarrels wrong? How can we tell which "battles" we need to fight?

2. How can we cultivate "God's kind of wisdom" in our lives?

3. What does Jas 4:2-3 have to say to us about our prayer life? Are we making the same mistakes in our prayers? How can we change?

GROUP REFLECTION

What is God saying to us as a group through Jas 3:13–4:3?

ACTION

What are we going to do, individually or as a group, in response to what God is saying to us?

PRAYER

How should we pray for each other in response to God's message to us in this passage?

Take turns talking to God about this passage and about what he is saying.

NEXT: JAMES 4:4-12 (The Root of the Matter: Spiritual Wholeness)

The Root of the Matter: Spiritual Wholeness

JAMES
4:4-12

OUTLINE

DAY **1** ◆ James 4:4

READING: **JAMES 4:4-12**
> Begin with prayer, asking God to give you insight, understanding, and an open heart to listen to and follow his word.

STUDY: **JAMES 4:4**
> Read the first part of the study note on Jas 4:4 and consult Isa 54:5-6; Jer 3:20; Hos 2:5-7. What is the significance of the label "adulterers" (literally "adulteresses") in the context of these OT passages?

> Why, then, does James call his readers "adulterers"?

> What exactly is "friendship with the world," and how is it opposed to friendship with God?

FURTHER STUDY (Optional)
> Read 1 Jn 2:15-17. What does this passage contribute to your understanding of Jas 4:4?

REFLECTION
> What does it really mean in practice to stop being a "friend of the world" and to be a friend of God?

> What do you think God is saying to you through your study of Jas 4:4?

PRAYER
> Talk to God about what you have read, any questions or concerns you might have, and what you think he might be saying to you today. You can write your prayer here if you wish.

DAY 2 ◆ James 4:5-6

READING: JAMES 4:4-12
Begin with prayer, asking God to give you insight, understanding, and an open heart to listen to and follow his word.

STUDY: JAMES 4:5-6
Read the study note on Jas 4:5, which suggests three different ways that the end of the verse could be translated. Which option do you think best fits the context? Why?

God desires us, and he allows evil to exist, but he doesn't actively cause evil for us

What point is James making in 4:5?

our spirits are naturally envious

The phrase "to stand against such evil desires" in Jas 4:6 is added to the text by the NLT to clarify the sense. In light of this phrase, what is 4:6 saying in relation to 4:5?

How does the quotation in Jas 4:6 from Prov 3:34 contribute to James's argument in these verses?

FURTHER STUDY (Optional)
The word translated "envy" in Jas 4:5 is found in the NT also (sometimes translated "jealousy") in Matt 27:18; Mark 15:10; Rom 1:29; Gal 5:21; Phil 1:15; 1 Tim 6:4; Titus 3:3; and 1 Pet 2:1. What do these other passages suggest about the meaning of the word here?

REFLECTION
How can our "envy" lead us to become "friends of the world" (Jas 4:4)?

What do you think God is saying to you through your study of Jas 4:5-6?

PRAYER

Talk to God about what you have read, any questions or concerns you might have, and what you think he might be saying to you today. You can write your prayer here if you wish.

DAY 3 ◆ James 4:7-8

READING: JAMES 4:4-12

Begin with prayer, asking God to give you insight, understanding, and an open heart to listen to and follow his word.

STUDY: JAMES 4:7-8

Jas 4:7-10 uses the technique of "bookending" the passage to tie it together. What, then, is the overall message of 4:7-10?

How does each of the commands in Jas 4:7-8 relate specifically to 4:5-6?

Why does James use the combination "hands" and "hearts" in 4:8?

FURTHER STUDY (Optional)

The Greek word that is translated in Jas 4:8 as "loyalty is divided" (*dipsuchos*, literally, "double-souled") is found elsewhere in the Bible only in Jas 1:8. What do these two passages have in common? What do they tell us about the theme of the letter?

REFLECTION

God promises that he will "come close" to those who "come close" to him. What does this mean for you in your life? *when I try to be close to God, I know that God will be close to me and help me*

What do you think God is saying to you through your study of Jas 4:7-8?

PRAYER

Talk to God about what you have read, any questions or concerns you might have, and what you think he might be saying to you today. You can write your prayer here if you wish.

DAY **4** ◆ James 4:9-10

READING: JAMES 4:4-12

Begin with prayer, asking God to give you insight, understanding, and an open heart to listen to and follow his word.

STUDY: JAMES 4:9-10

How do James's commands in 4:9 relate to Paul's command that we "always be full of joy in the Lord" (Phil 4:4)?

Read Luke 6:24-26, which is mentioned in the NLT Study Bible cross-references. How does this passage help you understand Jas 4:9?

How does the Lord "lift you up in honor" (Jas 4:10)? What is James referring to?

FURTHER STUDY (Optional)

Read 1 Pet 5:5-9. How does the passage in 1 Peter help in our understanding of the passage in James? And what do these parallels suggest about the teaching in Jas 4?

REFLECTION

What worldview is suggested by these commands in Jas 4:9-10? How does that worldview differ from the worldview of our culture?

What do you think God is saying to you through your study of Jas 4:9-10?

PRAYER
Talk to God about what you have read, any questions or concerns you might have, and what you think he might be saying to you today. You can write your prayer here if you wish.

DAY 5 ◆ James 4:11-12

READING: JAMES 4:4-12
Begin with prayer, asking God to give you insight, understanding, and an open heart to listen to and follow his word.

STUDY: JAMES 4:11-12
How does 4:11-12 fit in the immediate context of James? What relationship do these verses have to 3:13−4:10?

Why does our criticizing of one another involve criticizing God's law?

Why does James introduce the word "neighbor" at the end of 4:12?

FURTHER STUDY (Optional)
Read the passages mentioned in the study notes on Jas 4:11-12 (Lev 19:16-18; Matt 7:1-5; Luke 6:37; Jas 1:22-23). What do these passages teach, and how does it relate to the message of Jas 4:11-12?

REFLECTION

Reflect on the relationship between Jas 4:11 and 4:12. How does this relationship help us understand our critical attitudes toward one another? How should this verse help us overcome those attitudes?

What do you think God is saying to you through your study of Jas 4:11-12?

PRAYER

Talk to God about what you have read, any questions or concerns you might have, and what you think he might be saying to you today. You can write your prayer here if you wish.

GROUP SESSION

READING: JAMES 4:4-12

Read Jas 4:4-12 together as a group.

DISCUSSION

You can use the following questions to guide what you share in the discussion. Give each person at least one opportunity to share with the others.

What did you learn from Jas 4:4-12? What was one thing that stood out to you as you studied this passage? How did Jas 4:4-12 surprise you? Do you have questions about this passage or the study materials that haven't been answered? What does God seem to be saying to you through what you have studied?

TOPICS FOR DISCUSSION

You can choose from among these topics to generate a discussion among the members of your group, or you can write your thoughts about one or more of these topics if you're studying solo.

1. James condemns "friendship with the world." How can we be "salt and light" to the world (Matt 5:13-16) at the same time as we avoid becoming "friends" with the world?

2. James's claim that his readers are "adulterers" is a strong and sobering warning. What does this mean in practice? What form does this "adultery" take in our own life or in the Christian church in our day?

3. James urges us to "resist the devil" (4:7). How can we specifically do this in our day-to-day Christian lives?

GROUP REFLECTION

What is God saying to us as a group through Jas 4:4-12?

ACTION

What are we going to do, individually or as a group, in response to what God is saying to us?

PRAYER

How should we pray for each other in response to God's message to us in this passage?

Take turns talking to God about this passage and about what he is saying.

NEXT: JAMES 4:13–5:6 (**The Dangers of Arrogance and Greed**)

WEEK
TEN

*The Dangers
of Arrogance and
Greed*

JAMES
4:13–5:6

OUTLINE

DAY **1** ◆ James 4:13-14

READING: **JAMES 4:13-17**

Begin with prayer, asking God to give you insight, understanding, and an open heart to listen to and follow his word.

STUDY: **JAMES 4:13-14**

Read the study note on 4:13-16. What kind of people in our culture are like these itinerant merchants? What other kinds of people might harbor this same attitude?

businessmen, rich people, lawyers, those with money who think that life should follow their plans

As he does so often, James's teaching picks up key themes from the teaching of Jesus. Read Luke 12:15-21, which is mentioned in the NLT Study Bible cross-references. How are these two passages similar? What does Luke 12:15-21 add to our understanding of the theme of Jas 4:13-14? *someone successful makes plans for himself but dies and loses everything before they are realized*

REFLECTION

Ponder the reminder of James that "your life is like the morning fog." What issues in your own life does this reminder impact? *crises, triumphs, pain, pleasure, success, failure*

What do you think God is saying to you through your study of Jas 4:13-14?

PRAYER

Talk to God about what you have read, any questions or concerns you might have, and what you think he might be saying to you today. You can write your prayer here if you wish.

READING: JAMES 4:13-17

Begin with prayer, asking God to give you insight, understanding, and an open heart to listen to and follow his word.

STUDY: JAMES 4:15-17

James encourages his readers to say "If the Lord wants us to. . . ." What is James really getting at? *remember that God is truly in control of our lives and knows what will happen*

In 4:16, James refers to boasting "about your own plans" (or, "in your arrogance"). What kind of boasting is James talking about here? Can you think of examples of this kind of boasting that you have observed? *thinking that through their own planning, these people don't need God's help*

The study note on Jas 4:17 suggests that this verse may be a popular saying that James is applying to this specific situation. What does the saying contribute to our understanding of sin? *sin can both be active and passive, inaction can allow evil to appear*

FURTHER STUDY (Optional)

Read the passages listed in the study note on Jas 4:17 (Deut 24:15; Prov 3:27-28; Matt 25:41-46; Luke 12:47). How does each of these passages support the idea of the popular saying that James quotes?

REFLECTION

Is James condemning all forms of planning in this passage? It not, how can we distinguish between appropriate planning and boastful, evil planning? *no, making plans according to an understanding of what God wants is acceptable*

What do you think God is saying to you through your study of Jas 4:15-17?

Talk to God about what you have read, any questions or concerns you might have, and what you think he might be saying to you today. You can write your prayer here if you wish.

DAY 3 ◆ James 5:1

READING: JAMES 5:1-6

Begin with prayer, asking God to give you insight, understanding, and an open heart to listen to and follow his word.

STUDY: JAMES 5:1

James begins the paragraph 5:1-6 the same way that he began 4:13-17. What does this suggest about these two paragraphs? *both are addressed to arrogant sinners*

Are the "rich people" James is addressing genuine believers in Christ? Why or not? *no, they have cheated people and relied on their own wealth instead of God*

Read the following similar passages in the OT: Isa 13:6-10 and Amos 8:3. What are the "terrible troubles" that are coming to rich people? *God's wrath and judgment is coming on them*

FURTHER STUDY (Optional)

Consider the meaning of the word "rich" in Jas 5:1 in light of the usage of this word in some OT passages (Prov 10:15-16 and 14:20) and in the teaching of Jesus (Luke 6:24-26). What kind of people does James have in mind?

REFLECTION

James often warns about the judgment to come (see also 2:12-13; 4:12; 5:9). Why does James bring in this theme so often? How does it affect your understanding of the Christian life?

What do you think God is saying to you through your study of Jas 5:1?

PRAYER

Talk to God about what you have read, any questions or concerns you might have, and what you think he might be saying to you today. You can write your prayer here if you wish.

DAY 4 ◆ James 5:2-4

READING: JAMES 5:1-6

Begin with prayer, asking God to give you insight, understanding, and an open heart to listen to and follow his word.

STUDY: JAMES 5:2-4

James refers to "fine clothes," "gold and silver," and "treasure" as indicators of wealth. What are the indicators of wealth in your culture and circumstances?

cars, houses, latest fashions, flaunted wealth is jewlery or watches

Read the study notes on Jas 5:3-4. Why, according to this passage, will accumulated treasures stand as evidence against the rich on the day of judgment?

being miserly and hoarding wealth unjustly will destroy them

In 5:4, what does James mean by referring to God as "the LORD of Heaven's Armies" (cp. 1 Sam 17:45; Isa 5:9)?

the commander of the fury and power of heaven's warriors to show that he is to be feared by his enemies

FURTHER STUDY (Optional)

Read Deut 24:14-15. What does it teach? How does it confirm James's warnings here?

James was dependent on Jesus' teaching (see Matt 6:19). But James also picks up themes from Jewish literature. For example:

"Help a poor man for the commandment's sake, and because of his need do not send him away empty. Lose your silver for the sake of a brother or a friend, and do not let it rust under a stone and be lost. Lay up your treasure according to the commandments of the Most High, and it will profit you more than gold" (*Sirach* 29:9-11, RSV).

What does this passage add to our understanding of what James is saying here?

REFLECTION

James 5:4 reflects on the situation of a day laborer in his own culture who needed daily pay to buy food. What might be the contemporary equivalent of this kind of withholding of wages?

What do you think God is saying to you through your study of Jas 5:2-4?

PRAYER

Talk to God about what you have read, any questions or concerns you might have, and what you think he might be saying to you today. You can write your prayer here if you wish.

DAY 5 ◆ James 5:5-6

READING: JAMES 5:1-6

Begin with prayer, asking God to give you insight, understanding, and an open heart to listen to and follow his word.

STUDY: JAMES 5:5-6

The Greek behind "spent your years . . . in luxury" is found elsewhere in the Bible only in 1 Tim 5:6 and in the Old Greek translation of Ezek 16:49. Read these passages. What do they contribute to your understanding of Jas 5:5?

What, in this context, does "the day of slaughter" refer to?

when God will bring down the rich and proud

What does the claim at the end of Jas 5:6 that the innocent people "do not resist you" add to James's argument? *they take advantage of the defenseless who cannot resist them*

FURTHER STUDY (Optional)

Jesus also warned the rich—for example, read Luke 16:19-31. What similarities do you see between the warnings of Jesus and James?

In what ways do rich people condemn and kill "innocent people"? (Note Jas 2:6 and especially 1 Kgs 21:1-16.)

REFLECTION

James condemns people for living in luxury on this earth. What does living "in luxury" look like in our day? Is James condemning anyone who lives at a certain lifestyle level? How can we know if this condemnation applies to us?

What do you think God is saying to you through your study of Jas 5:5-6?

PRAYER

Talk to God about what you have read, any questions or concerns you might have, and what you think he might be saying to you today. You can write your prayer here if you wish.

GROUP SESSION

READING: JAMES 4:13–5:6

Read Jas 4:13–5:6 together as a group.

DISCUSSION

You can use the following questions to guide what you share in the discussion. Give each person at least one opportunity to share with the others.

What did you learn from Jas 4:13–5:6? What was one thing that stood out to you as you studied this passage? How did Jas 4:13–5:6 surprise you? Do you have questions about this passage or the study materials that haven't been answered? What does God seem to be saying to you through what you have studied?

TOPICS FOR DISCUSSION

You can choose from among these topics to generate a discussion among the members of your group, or you can write your thoughts about one or more of these topics if you're studying solo.

1. What general theme binds together the two paragraphs, Jas 4:13-17 and 5:1-6? What can be learned from James's association of these two?

2. Is the condemnation that James pronounces in 5:1-6 applicable to all "rich people"? Why or why not? And what does "rich" mean in our own context?

3. Jas 5:1-6 contains the strongest denunciation of "rich people" in the NT. What does this denunciation have to do with believers in Christ? How should those of us who live in wealthy cultures respond to this denunciation?

GROUP REFLECTION

What is God saying to us as a group through Jas 4:13–5:6?

ACTION

What are we going to do, individually or as a group, in response to what God is saying to us?

PRAYER

How should we pray for each other in response to God's message to us in this passage?

Take turns talking to God about this passage and about what he is saying.

NEXT: JAMES 5:7-12 (**Enduring until the Coming of the Lord**)

Enduring
until the Coming
of the Lord

JAMES
5:7-12

OUTLINE

DAY **1** ◆ James 5:7

READING: **JAMES 5:7-12**
> Begin with prayer, asking God to give you insight, understanding, and an open heart to listen to and follow his word.

STUDY: **JAMES 5:7**
> How does the audience of this paragraph contrast with the audience of 4:13–5:6? (See also the study note on 5:7-8.)

> What does James mean by "the Lord's return"? Read "The Future Coming of the Lord (5:7-9)," p. 2119. What does James teach about this event?

> As James encourages his readers to "be patient" in waiting for the Lord's return, he draws an analogy with the way farmers "patiently wait for the rains." This analogy has Old Testament parallels (see Deut 11:14; Jer 5:24; Hos 6:3; Joel 2:23; Zech 10:1). What does this analogy teach Christians who are waiting for the Lord's return?

FURTHER STUDY (Optional)
> Read Ps 37. What are the similarities between this psalm and Jas 5:1-11? How does the psalm help us understand what James is teaching?

> The word "return" (Greek *parousia*) is defined in the *NLT Study Bible* word study dictionary as "the presence of a person in a particular place with a focus on the event of the person's arrival. In the NT the word often refers to the future coming of Jesus Christ in glory." Also read Matt 24:3, 37; 1 Cor 15:23; 1 Thes 3:13; 4:15; 5:23; 2 Pet 3:4; 1 Jn 2:28.

> Why do Christians await the arrival and presence of Jesus Christ "eagerly" but "patiently"? In the context of this passage, what does the arrival of Jesus promise to bring?

REFLECTION

What is the patience that James calls us on to exhibit here? (Cp. Jas 5:10-11.) What does such patience look like in everyday life?

What do you think God is saying to you through your study of Jas 5:7?

PRAYER

Talk to God about what you have read, any questions or concerns you might have, and what you think he might be saying to you today. You can write your prayer here if you wish.

DAY 2 ◆ James 5:8-9

READING: JAMES 5:7-12

Begin with prayer, asking God to give you insight, understanding, and an open heart to listen to and follow his word.

STUDY: JAMES 5:8-9

In what ways is the farmer a good illustration of patience in the face of difficulty?

Why, in this context, does James warn believers about "grumbling" against each other?

When James claims that "the coming of the Lord is near" (cp. Mark 1:15; Rom 13:12; 1 Pet 4:7), what does he mean?

FURTHER STUDY (Optional)

"Take courage" reflects a Greek verb that is also used in Luke 22:32; Rom 1:11; 16:25; 1 Thes 3:2, 13; 2 Thes 2:17; 3:3; 1 Pet 5:10; 2 Pet 1:12; Rev 3:2. Look up these other verses. How would you describe what James is calling for here?

How can we put into practice what James is calling us to do in this passage?

What do you think God is saying to you through your study of Jas 5:8-9?

PRAYER

Talk to God about what you have read, any questions or concerns you might have, and what you think he might be saying to you today. You can write your prayer here if you wish.

DAY 3 ◆ James 5:10

READING: JAMES 5:7-12

Begin with prayer, asking God to give you insight, understanding, and an open heart to listen to and follow his word.

STUDY: JAMES 5:10

The study note on Jas 5:10 suggests that the verse "reflects on" Matt 5:11 and Luke 6:23. How is James's instruction here a reflection on those verses?

Why does James remind us that the prophets "spoke in the name of the Lord"? What does this reminder add to our understanding and application of 5:10?

FURTHER STUDY (Optional)

Read Heb 11:1-40, a passage that provides many examples of "prophets who spoke in the name of the Lord" and endured great difficulty. What do their examples teach you about patience in suffering?

REFLECTION

Who else have left you an example that has had a strong impact on your spiritual life?

What do you think God is saying to you through your study of Jas 5:10?

PRAYER

Talk to God about what you have read, any questions or concerns you might have, and what you think he might be saying to you today. You can write your prayer here if you wish.

DAY 4 ◆ James 5:11

READING: JAMES 5:7-12

Begin with prayer, asking God to give you insight, understanding, and an open heart to listen to and follow his word.

STUDY: JAMES 5:11

The Greek word translated "We give great honor" could also be translated "We count as blessed." How does this alternative translation alter the meaning of the passage?

Read Job 1:20-22; 2:7-10. In what sense did Job "endure" under suffering? (See also the study note on Jas 5:11.)

What point is James making by referring to the example of Job?

What do Job 3:1-26; 12:1-3; 16:1-3, 19-21; 19:25-27 teach us about Job's "endurance"?

REFLECTION
What does Job's example of endurance teach us about enduring our own suffering?

What do you think God is saying to you through your study of Jas 5:11?

PRAYER
Talk to God about what you have read, any questions or concerns you might have, and what you think he might be saying to you today. You can write your prayer here if you wish.

DAY 5 ◆ James 5:12

READING: JAMES 5:7-12
Begin with prayer, asking God to give you insight, understanding, and an open heart to listen to and follow his word.

STUDY: JAMES 5:12
Why does James introduce here the point about not taking oaths?

James introduces this verse with "But most of all." Note a similar phrase in 1 Pet 4:8. Why does James introduce 5:12 in this way? What is he saying?

Read the study note on Jas 5:12. What exactly was James prohibiting, and what was he not prohibiting?

James refers to Jesus' teaching throughout his letter, but this verse is the closest verbal parallel to Jesus' teaching (see Matt 5:34-37). What is Jesus teaching in Matt 5:34-37?

How does Matt 5:34-37 shed light on what James is saying in 5:12?

REFLECTION

How in practice should we implement the prohibition of this verse? What situations in our day would it relate to?

What do you think God is saying to you through your study of Jas 5:12?

PRAYER

Talk to God about what you have read, any questions or concerns you might have, and what you think he might be saying to you today. You can write your prayer here if you wish.

GROUP SESSION

READING: **JAMES 5:7-12**

Read Jas 5:7-12 together as a group.

DISCUSSION

You can use the following questions to guide what you share in the discussion. Give each person at least one opportunity to share with the others.

What did you learn from Jas 5:7-12? What was one thing that stood out to you as you studied this passage? How did Jas 5:7-12 surprise you? Do you have questions about this passage or the study materials that haven't been answered? What does God seem to be saying to you through what you have studied?

TOPICS FOR DISCUSSION

You can choose from among these topics to generate a discussion among the members of your group, or you can write your thoughts about one or more of these topics if you're studying solo.

1. James encourages his readers to respond to their poverty and difficulties with "patience." Does this mean that oppressed people should never rise up against their oppressors? How should this teaching be put into effect in our modern societies?

2. James refers to the "nearness" of the Lord's coming as an incentive for right living. How, after twenty centuries of waiting for his coming, can we continue to let the Lord's coming motivate us toward faithful Christian living?

GROUP REFLECTION

What is God saying to us as a group through Jas 5:7-12?

ACTION

What are we going to do, individually or as a group, in response to what God is saying to us?

PRAYER

How should we pray for each other in response to God's message to us in this passage?

Take turns talking to God about this passage and about what he is saying.

NEXT: JAMES 5:13-20 (Helping One Another)

WEEK

TWELVE

Helping One Another

JAMES
5:13-20

OUTLINE

DAY 1 . . . James 5:13-14

DAY 2 . . . James 5:15

DAY 3 . . . James 5:16

DAY 4 . . . James 5:17-18

DAY 5 . . . James 5:19-20

Group Session

DAY **1** ◆ James 5:13-14

READING: JAMES 5:13-20
>
> Begin with prayer, asking God to give you insight, understanding, and an open heart to listen to and follow his word.

STUDY: JAMES 5:13-14
>
> James instructs his readers how to respond to three different types of situations. What do the three kinds of responses have in common?
>
>
> Compare Jas 5:13 with Col 3:16-17. What similarities are there between James's teaching here and Paul's teaching in his letter to the Colossians?
>
>
> The study note on Jas 5:14 briefly explains the role of elders in the church. Why does James instruct his readers to go to the elders for prayer?
>
>
> Read the last part of the study note on Jas 5:14 and the associated cross-references (Isa 1:6; Matt 6:17; Mark 6:13; Luke 10:34). What is the significance of using oil in Jas 5:14?

FURTHER STUDY (Optional)
>
> The Greek Bible uses two different verbs for the English "anoint": *chrio* and *aleipho*. The former verb is used in Luke 4:18 [=Isa 61:1]; Acts 4:27; 10:38; 2 Cor 1:21 ["commissioned"]; Heb 1:9 [=Ps 45:7], while the latter is used in Matt 6:17; Mark 6:13; 16:1; Luke 7:38, 46; John 11:2; 12:3. What does James's use of the latter verb (*aleipho*) suggest about the meaning of "anoint with oil"?

REFLECTION
>
> Which of the kinds of situations that James addresses is your current experience closest to? How can you respond to it in a way that fits with James's instructions?

What do you think God is saying to you through your study of Jas 5:13-14?

PRAYER

Talk to God about what you have read, any questions or concerns you might have, and what you think he might be saying to you today. You can write your prayer here if you wish.

DAY 2 ◆ James 5:15

READING: JAMES 5:13-20

Begin with prayer, asking God to give you insight, understanding, and an open heart to listen to and follow his word.

STUDY: JAMES 5:15

What sort of prayer is a prayer "offered in faith"? (See the study note on 5:15.)

The Greek verb behind "will heal" can also mean "save" (see, e.g., Jas 1:21; 2:14; compare its use in Matt 8:25; 14:30; 27:40; Acts 27:20, 31; Jude 1:5). Is James talking about eternal salvation, or something else? Why has the NLT translated the verb "heal" here?

How can James promise that the sins of the sick person will be forgiven?

FURTHER STUDY (Optional)

Read the study note on Jas 5:15 and then also read John 9:1-3 and 1 Cor 11:27-30. What should we conclude about the NT teaching on the connection between sin and sickness?

REFLECTION

How can you offer prayers with true faith?

What do you think God is saying to you through your study of Jas 5:15?

PRAYER
Talk to God about what you have read, any questions or concerns you might have, and what you think he might be saying to you today. You can write your prayer here if you wish.

DAY 3 ◆ James 5:16

READING: JAMES 5:13-20
Begin with prayer, asking God to give you insight, understanding, and an open heart to listen to and follow his word.

STUDY: JAMES 5:16
Refer back to the study note on Jas 5:15. Why does prayer for healing also involve confession of sin?

When James refers to a "righteous person," does he mean a specially gifted or mature Christian, or any Christian?

The phrase "produces wonderful results" could also be translated "when it is empowered." What would this alternate translation add or change about James's teaching on prayer?

REFLECTION
Should believers confess sins to other believers? What sins, and to whom?

What do you think God is saying to you through your study of Jas 5:16?

PRAYER

Talk to God about what you have read, any questions or concerns you might have, and what you think he might be saying to you today. You can write your prayer here if you wish.

DAY 4 ◆ James 5:17-18

READING: JAMES 5:13-20

Begin with prayer, asking God to give you insight, understanding, and an open heart to listen to and follow his word.

STUDY: JAMES 5:17-18

What does James's reminder that Elijah was "as human as we are" contribute to his point?

Why might James have chosen this particular illustration of prayer in this context?

Read the study note on Jas 5:17. Why might James have wanted to use "three and a half years" (symbolizing "a period of judgment") in this context?

FURTHER STUDY (Optional)

Read the entire Elijah narrative that James alludes to here: 1 Kgs 17–18. What further can we learn about prayer and God's power from the whole passage?

REFLECTION

Why could Elijah, "human as we are," produce such great results by his praying when we often appear to accomplish so little?

What do you think God is saying to you through your study of Jas 5:17-18?

PRAYER

Talk to God about what you have read, any questions or concerns you might have, and what you think he might be saying to you today. You can write your prayer here if you wish.

DAY 5 ♦ James 5:19-20

READING: JAMES 5:13-20

Begin with prayer, asking God to give you insight, understanding, and an open heart to listen to and follow his word.

STUDY: JAMES 5:19-20

In what ways do these verses form a fitting conclusion to the letter of James?

Why has James used the particular expression "wanders away from the truth" here (instead of, for example, "sins")? What is he saying about this person?

What does James's claim that a wandering church member might be saved from (spiritual) "death" suggest about that person? How is your answer affected by your view of salvation?

FURTHER STUDY (Optional)

At the end of 5:20, James says that bringing a sinner back from death will "bring about the forgiveness of many sins." Whose sins might be in view here? Consult Prov 10:12 (which James might be referring to) and also Ezek 3:21; 1 Tim 4:16.

REFLECTION
What is your own response to James's encouragement in 5:19-20? What particular sins that James has talked about are affecting believers that you know?

What do you think God is saying to you through your study of Jas 5:19-20?

PRAYER
Talk to God about what you have read, any questions or concerns you might have, and what you think he might be saying to you today. You can write your prayer here if you wish.

GROUP SESSION

READING: **JAMES 5:13-20**
Read Jas 5:13-20 together as a group.

DISCUSSION
You can use the following questions to guide what you share in the discussion. Give each person at least one opportunity to share with the others.

What did you learn from Jas 5:13-20? What was one thing that stood out to you as you studied this passage? How did Jas 5:13-20 surprise you? Do you have questions about this passage or the study materials that haven't been answered? What does God seem to be saying to you through what you have studied?

TOPICS FOR DISCUSSION

You can choose from among these topics to generate a discussion among the members of your group, or you can write your thoughts about one or more of these topics if you're studying solo.

1. Read again the study note on Jas 5:15. Do you agree that only God can give the faith needed to activate prayers for healing? If so, what does this verse teach about the healing ministry of the church? What should our practice of praying for the sick look like?

2. In 5:16, James encourages believers to confess sins to one another and pray for each other. Are you doing this with other believers? Why is it important? How can local churches ensure that this kind of ministry is taking place?

3. How can the church do a better job of bringing back Christians who "wander away from the truth" (5:19-20)?

GROUP REFLECTION

What is God saying to us as a group through Jas 5:13-20?

ACTION

What are we going to do, individually or as a group, in response to what God is saying to us?

PRAYER

How should we pray for each other in response to God's message to us in this passage?

Take turns talking to God about this passage and about what he is saying.

THE LETTER OF JAMES

THE LETTER OF
JAMES

How can we be faithful friends of God like Abraham? Can we resist the pressures of the world, our rebellious human impulses, and the influence of the devil? Can Christians live together in peace as we seek solutions to life's problems? James addresses these issues in his letter as he seeks to motivate Christians to develop a mature and consistent faith and to show how Christians can have loyal friendship with God and with one another.

SETTING

James, Jesus' brother, writes as the leader of the Jerusalem church to Jewish Christians who have been scattered by persecution. He encourages them to endure their trials with Christian fortitude and to exhibit consistent Christian character.

The recipients of this letter were Jewish Christians (1:1; 2:1) who had been scattered by the persecutions which began with the stoning of Stephen (Acts 8:1; 11:19). They lived among the Jews who had been "scattered abroad" in the Diaspora (1:1; John 7:35), which had its origins in the Assyrian dispersion of Israel (the northern kingdom) in 722–721 BC and in the Babylonian exile of Judah (the southern kingdom) in 586 BC. This dispersion later included many Jews who traveled extensively during the Greek and Roman empires (4:13; Acts 13:14; 17:1). By the middle of the first century, there were Jewish communities all over the Greco-Roman world.

SUMMARY

The letter of James is written with a pastor's perspective, and it focuses more on ethics than any other book of the NT. The letter contains teachings based on the law as understood through the life and teaching of Jesus (1:25; 2:8). James also reflects Jesus' own teachings, especially as later recorded in Matthew's "Sermon on the Mount" (Matt 5–7) and Luke's "Sermon on the Plain" (Luke 6:20-49).

AUTHORSHIP

The letter of James was written by one of Jesus' brothers (see further "James, the Brother of Jesus" at Acts 15:13-21, p. 1858). Like the other sons of Joseph and Mary (Matt 13:55), James (Greek *Iakōbos*) bore the name of an Israelite hero: Jacob (Hebrew *Ya'aqob*; Greek *Iakōb*). After Jesus' resur-

◀ **The Setting of James, about AD 46.** James, one of Jesus' brothers, was a leader of the church in JERUSALEM. The believers from Jerusalem had been scattered in the early 40s AD as a result of persecution (see Acts 8:1-3; 12:1-4). The scattered believers traveled throughout JUDEA, SAMARIA, and PHOENICIA, and to ANTIOCH in SYRIA and CYPRUS (see Acts 11:19).

rection, James became a believer (cp. 1 Cor 15:7) and rose to a position of leadership in the Jerusalem church (see Acts 15:13-22).

During Jesus' public ministry, neither James nor the other siblings were followers of Jesus. They had even tried to end his ministry and bring him home to his responsibilities as eldest son (Mark 3:31-35; cp. John 7:3-5). A personal resurrection appearance convinced James that Jesus was the Christ (1 Cor 15:7), and he was with the others in the upper room when the Spirit was given on Pentecost (Acts 1:14; 2:1-3). James became the leader of the Jerusalem church after Peter's arrest and departure from Jerusalem (Acts 12:1-3; 15:13-21; 21:18; Gal 1:19; 2:9).

DATE AND LOCATION OF WRITING

The letter of James is one of the earliest books in the NT, written after the persecution under Herod Agrippa (AD 44, Acts 12:1-5), yet prior to Galatians (AD 48~49) and the council in Jerusalem (AD 49~50). It reflects an early period prior to the conflict over circumcising Gentile converts and before the development of false teachings in other Christian communities. It was a time when *synagogue* ("meeting," 2:2) and *church* (5:14) were interchangeable terms, as were *law* and *word* (1:23, 25).

That this letter was written from Jerusalem is deduced from information in Acts and Galatians about James's location (Acts 15:13-22; 21:18; Gal 1:18-19; 2:9, 12). The book contains allusions appropriate to Palestine, including references to the scorching heat (1:11); salty water springs (3:11); the cultivation of figs, olives, and grapevines (3:12); the imagery of the sea (1:6; 3:4); and the early and later rains (5:7).

LITERARY CHARACTER

The letter of James is written in good Koiné Greek, the common Greek of the Greco-Roman world. It reflects the Hellenistic influences on Galilee and Palestine, as well as the enculturation of Jewish readers in the Diaspora. James writes with grammatical accuracy, has a wide vocabulary, and has an elegant feel for the rhythms and sounds of words. There are clear allusions to the Greek translation of the OT (e.g., 4:6), with some imagery from the Hellenistic world.

James uses many oratorical devices, such as fraternal appeals (1:2; 2:1; 3:1; 4:11), rhetorical questions (2:5; 3:11-12; 4:1), imperative exhortations (1:16; 3:1; 5:16), metaphors and illustrations (2:26; 3:3-5; 4:14), and aphorisms that summarize a paragraph (2:13, 17; 3:18; 4:17).

James distinctively emphasizes friendship as the ideal relationship with God.

WILLIAM R. BAKER
Personal Speech-Ethics in the Epistle of James,
p. 288

[James] takes us . . . back to the infancy of the Christian Church, to the purple dawn of Christian enthusiasm and the first glow of Christian love.

J. B. ADAMSON
The Epistle of James, p. 21

MEANING AND MESSAGE

James's primary concern is for his readers to maintain undivided faith and loyalty toward God (1:6). They were under pressure from a society that oppressed them economically (2:6) and abused them for their faith in Jesus Christ (2:7). James recommends patient endurance (1:3), submission to God (4:7), and sharing in the ministries of the church (5:13-20). These will result in perfection (1:4), honor (4:10), and a glorious life (1:12) at the coming of Jesus Christ (5:8).

The Law. As leader of the Jerusalem church, James maintained proper respect for the law of Moses and for Jewish traditions, such as the purification ceremonies after a vow (Acts 21:18-25). James also expressed a sympathetic understanding of the Gentile mission when he concluded that Gentiles could be recognized as Christians without first becoming proselytes to Judaism. He based this on God's covenant with Noah (Acts 15:19-22; see Gen 9:1-17). In his letter, we find James both upholding the law (1:25) and at the same time hinting at its reinterpretation through Jesus the Messiah (2:8-11).

Jewishness. This is one of the most Jewish letters in the NT. James uses the symbols of Judaism with little criticism (contrast Matt 5:21-22) and uses the primary identity markers of Judaism without redefinition (contrast Rom 2:29). James addresses the readers as the "twelve tribes" (1:1) and identifies their church gathering as a synagogue (2:2) with its elders (5:14) and teachers (3:1). He refers to the law of Moses repeatedly (1:25; 2:8-12; 4:11), cites the foundational creed of Israel (the *Shema,* 2:19), and names God as "the Lord of Heaven's Armies" (5:4), a common OT title for God. James also uses the literary elements of OT wisdom literature (1:5; 3:13, 17) and prophetic exhortations (4:13; 5:1). He appeals to Israel's heroes (Abraham, 2:21, 23; Rahab, 2:25; Job, 5:11; Elijah, 5:17). He does not, however, explicitly mention the ceremonial elements of Judaism, such as the Sabbath, circumcision, or food laws.

Works. The apparent differences between James and Paul regarding "good works" must be understood in their differing historical and theological contexts. Paul emphasized that people could not get right with God by "obeying the law" (Rom 3:20, 28; Gal 2:16) or, indeed by anything that they might do (Rom 4:3-5). Only God, through his initiative of grace, could overcome the problem of human sin; a person must respond to him by faith. Both Paul and James believed this, but they differed in their emphasis. Paul emphasized that works of the law do not produce salvation (Eph 2:8-9), and so he opposed circumcision of Gentiles (Rom 4:5; Gal 2:11-12; 5:2-6).

James, however, was addressing Jewish Christian communities. He speaks of "good works" as charitable deeds (2:14-18, 21-24). Good deeds are faithful obedience; they are the evidence of a genuine relationship with God based on faith. True biblical faith will always produce good deeds pleasing to God. James emphasizes that faith cannot be reduced to a mere affirmation of truth (2:19), and faithfulness does not allow for divided allegiance between God and the world (1:8; 4:4, 7).

The letter of James gives us insight into very early communities of Christian Jews. It also helps us understand how Christians should live when they are a minority group in the midst of an oppressive, non-Christian society. It is alive with godly counsel for us today.

FURTHER READING
LUKE TIMOTHY JOHNSON
James (1995)
RALPH MARTIN
James (1989)
DOUGLAS J. MOO
James (2000)

1:2-3
1 Pet 1:6-7

1:4
ªteleios (5046)
▸ Jas 3:2

1:5
Prov 2:3-6
Matt 7:7

1:6
Matt 21:22

1:10-11
Isa 40:6-7
1 Pet 1:24

1:12
Rev 2:10; 3:11
ᵇmakarios (3107)
▸ 1 Pet 3:14
ᶜpeirasmos (3986)
▸ Jas 1:13

1:13
ᵈpeirazō (3985)
▸ 1 Pet 4:12

1:14
Prov 19:3

1:15
ᵉhamartia (0266)
▸ Jas 5:15

1:16
1 Cor 6:9

1:17
Gen 1:16
Ps 136:7
Matt 7:11
ᶠpatēr (3962)
▸ 1 Jn 2:13

1:18
John 1:13
1 Pet 1:23

1. GREETINGS FROM JAMES (1:1)

1 This letter is from James, a slave of God and of the Lord Jesus Christ.

I am writing to the "twelve tribes"—Jewish believers scattered abroad. Greetings!

2. FAITH AND ENDURANCE (1:2-18)

²Dear brothers and sisters, when troubles come your way, consider it an opportunity for great joy. ³For you know that when your faith is tested, your endurance has a chance to grow. ⁴So let it grow, for when your endurance is ªfully developed, you will be ªperfect and complete, needing nothing.

⁵If you need wisdom, ask our generous God, and he will give it to you. He will not rebuke you for asking. ⁶But when you ask him, be sure that your faith is in God alone. Do not waver, for a person with divided loyalty is as unsettled as a wave of the sea that is blown and tossed by the wind. ⁷Such people should not expect to receive anything from the Lord. ⁸Their loyalty is divided between God and the world, and they are unstable in everything they do.

⁹Believers who are poor have something to boast about, for God has honored them. ¹⁰And those who are rich should boast that God has humbled them. They will fade away like a little flower in the field. ¹¹The hot sun rises and the grass withers; the little flower droops and falls, and its beauty fades away. In the same way, the rich will fade away with all of their achievements.

¹²God ᵇblesses those who patiently endure ᶜtesting and temptation. Afterward they will receive the crown of life that God has promised to those who love him. ¹³And remember, when you are being ᵈtempted, do not say, "God is ᵈtempting me." God is never tempted to do wrong, and he never ᵈtempts anyone else. ¹⁴Temptation comes from our own desires, which entice us and drag us away. ¹⁵These desires give birth to ᵉsinful actions. And when ᵉsin is allowed to grow, it gives birth to death.

¹⁶So don't be misled, my dear brothers and sisters. ¹⁷Whatever is good and perfect comes down to us from God our ᶠFather, who created all the lights in the heavens. He never changes or casts a shifting shadow. ¹⁸He chose to give birth to us by giving us his true word. And we, out of all creation, became his prized possession.

1:1 James: See "James, the Brother of Jesus" at Acts 15:13-21, p. 1588. • By identifying his readers as the "twelve tribes," James affirms Christianity's continuity with Israel's heritage. The Exile had dispersed the twelve tribes, but Jewish interpreters looked forward to God reuniting them (see Psalms of Solomon 17:26-28; Testament of Benjamin 9:2; cp. Ezek 37:15-28; Matt 19:28). Christ has spiritually brought an end to Israel's exile and reunited the tribes. • Jews scattered abroad (Greek diaspora) were living outside Palestine (John 7:35; Acts 2:5; 8:1; 11:19). • Greetings! (Greek chairein): This greeting is typical in first-century Greek letters (Acts 15:23; 23:26) and interpersonally (Matt 26:49; Luke 1:28).

1:2-4 Enduring troubles and temptations is a recurring theme (1:12-15; 5:7-12). Failure to endure is "wandering from the truth" that requires being "saved from death" (5:19-20).

1:2 Dear brothers and sisters: Literally My brothers; also in 1:16, 19. See note on 2:1. • James uses a wordplay: joy (Greek chara) in 1:2 is related to greetings in 1:1.

1:5-8 James introduces wisdom as a recurring theme (cp. 3:13-18).

1:6 Do not waver, for a person with divided loyalty: The Greek is often translated Do not doubt, for a person who doubts, but the sense here is of a person whose loyalty is divided between God and the world (see 1:8).

1:8 Their loyalty is divided between God

and the world (literally They are double-minded): James might have created the Greek word used here. He emphasizes the need for confidence in God alone.

1:9-11 Poverty and wealth are a recurring theme (cp. 2:1-26; 4:13–5:11). James does not promise material wealth to the righteous poor but announces a future reversal in heaven.

1:9 Believers who are: Literally The brother who is; see note on 2:1. • something to boast about: In the NT, boasting is usually viewed negatively (3:14; 4:16; Eph 2:9), but here it means boasting about what God has done (2:5; Rom 15:18; 1 Cor 1:31; Gal 6:14).

1:10 those who are rich should boast: With irony, James is describing the dreadful fate of the ungodly rich who elevate themselves by oppressing poor and vulnerable people (see 2:6-8; 5:1-6).

1:12-27 James addresses the same three topics as in 1:2-11, adding a new dimension to each topic. External testing (1:2-4) becomes internal temptation (1:11-18); the need for wisdom (1:5-8) is related to controlling angry speech (1:19-21); and poverty/wealth relate to the need to act upon God's word (1:22-25). The section then summarizes these themes (1:26-27).

1:12 Those who love him are faithful and obedient (cp. 1:22-25; 2:5; Deut 7:9; 1 Jn 5:2).

1:13 do not say: James is using diatribe, in which an imaginary opponent presents a contrary opinion. In this way he is able

to voice the readers' possible objection and immediately refute it (also in 2:3, 16, 18; 4:13). • God is never tempted to do wrong: Or God should not be put to a test by evil people; the alternate translation dulls the parallelism with he never tempts.

1:14 Like hooks for fishing or traps for hunting, desires . . . entice us into sin and drag us away from faithfulness to God.

1:15 When evil desires conceive, they give birth to sinful actions (literally sin, personified as an infant). When the infant sin is allowed to grow to full maturity, it gives birth to death, in opposition to "the crown of [eternal] life" (1:12).

1:17 from God our Father, who created all the lights in the heavens (literally from above, from the Father of lights): God is the Father of lights since he created everything in the heavens (Gen 1:3, 14-17). In contrast to the moving lights in the heavens, God never changes or casts a shifting shadow (some manuscripts read He never changes, as a shifting shadow does).

1:18 God's true word is the Good News (1:21-23; 1 Pet 1:23-25). • give birth: The imagery of a mother giving birth shows the full scope of God's parental love for his children (cp. Luke 13:34; John 1:13; 3:3-8; 1 Pet 1:23). • we, out of all creation, became his prized possession: Literally we became a kind of firstfruit of his creatures (cp. Exod 23:16; Lev 23:9-14; 1 Cor 15:20; Col 1:18). Christians are examples of the ultimate restoration of all creation (Rom 8:20-22).

3. LISTENING AND DOING (1:19-27)

[19]Understand this, my dear brothers and sisters: You must all be quick to listen, slow to speak, and slow to get angry. [20]Human anger does not produce the righteousness God desires. [21]So get rid of all the filth and evil in your lives, and humbly accept the word God has planted in your hearts, for it has the power to save your souls.

[22]But don't just listen to God's word. You must do what it says. Otherwise, you are only fooling yourselves. [23]For if you listen to the word and don't obey, it is like glancing at your face in a mirror. [24]You see yourself, walk away, and forget what you look like. [25]But if you look carefully into the perfect [g]law that sets you [h]free, and if you do what it says and don't forget what you heard, then God will bless you for doing it.

[26]If you claim to be religious but don't control your tongue, you are fooling yourself, and your religion is [i]worthless. [27]Pure and genuine religion in the sight of God the Father means caring for orphans and widows in their distress and refusing to let the world corrupt you.

4. POVERTY AND GENEROSITY (2:1-26)

A Warning against Prejudice

2 My dear brothers and sisters, how can you claim to have faith in our glorious Lord Jesus Christ if you favor some people over others?

[2]For example, suppose someone comes into your [j]meeting dressed in fancy clothes and expensive jewelry, and another comes in who is poor and dressed in dirty clothes. [3]If you give special attention and a good seat to the rich person, but you say to the poor one, "You can stand over there, or else sit on the floor"—well, [4]doesn't this discrimination show that your judgments are guided by evil motives?

[5]Listen to me, dear brothers and sisters. Hasn't God chosen the poor in this world to be rich in faith? Aren't they the ones who will inherit the Kingdom he promised to those who love him? [6]But you dishonor the poor! Isn't it the rich who oppress you and drag you into court? [7]Aren't they the ones who slander Jesus Christ, whose noble name you bear?

[8]Yes indeed, it is good when you obey the royal law as found in the Scriptures: "Love

1:19
Prov 10:19; 15:1
1:21
Eph 1:31; 4:22
Col 1:28
1 Pet 2:1
1:22
Matt 7:21, 26
Rom 2:13
1:25
John 13:17
1 Pet 2:16
[g]*nomos* (3551)
▸ Jas 2:10
[h]*eleutheria* (1657)
▸ Jas 2:12
1:26
Ps 34:13
[i]*mataios* (3152)
▸ 1 Pet 1:18
2:1
Prov 24:23
Acts 10:34
1 Cor 2:8
2:2
[j]*sunagōgē* (4864)
▸ Rev 1:20
2:4
John 7:23-24
2:5
Luke 6:20; 21:1-4
1 Cor 1:26-28
2:7
Acts 11:26
1 Pet 4:16
2:8
*Lev 19:18
Matt 7:12
Rom 13:8

. . . .

1:20 *Human anger:* Literally *A man's anger.* • *the righteousness:* Or *the justice.*

1:21 *get rid of:* Literally *put off,* like filthy clothing; cp. Eph 4:22; 1 Pet 2:1. • *the word God has planted . . . has the power to save your souls:* James emphasizes that Christians are called to respond to a word that God himself has put within our very beings (in fulfillment of Jer 31:31-34). • The soul refers to the whole person (so also in 5:20; see Gen 2:7; 1 Pet 3:20).

1:22-23 In several places, James appears to be reflecting on Jesus' teachings. These verses reflect the teaching of Jesus (Matt 7:24, 26; Luke 6:46, 49).

1:22 *don't just listen to God's word:* Reading the scriptures was an important part of worship (Luke 4:16-17; Acts 13:13-16; Col 4:16; 1 Tim 4:13). Since most people could not read and copies were not readily available, they listened to the readings in public worship.

1:24 *forget what you look like:* The problem is not the poor quality of an ancient mirror but the inattention of the viewer (cp. Matt 7:24-27).

1:25 *law that sets you free:* God's word gives us new birth and salvation (1:18, 21) but demands that we *do what it says* (1:22-25).

1:26-27 *control* (literally *bridle*) *your tongue:* James uses the graphic image of the bridle in a horse's mouth to imply the relationship between speech and a whole body of behaviors (cp. 3:1-13).

• *Orphans and widows* were the most helpless members of ancient society. They were dependent upon the care of others, since the husband and father was the means of economic support and social contact (Exod 22:22-24; Deut 10:18). Christians are called to take care of the helpless (cp. 1 Tim 5:3-16). • In James, *the world* stands in opposition to God (cp. 3:15; 4:4; Rom 12:2; 1 Jn 2:15-17).

2:1-4 James gives a realistic illustration to enforce his prohibition against favoring the wealthy.

2:1 *dear brothers and sisters* (literally *brothers;* also in 2:5, 14): The Greek word used here means *fellow Christians* of either sex. James frequently begins a new section with this affectionate greeting (1:2, 16; 2:14; 3:1; 5:7, 19), soliciting their loyal response. • James contrasts *our glorious Lord Jesus Christ* with the glory of a well-dressed man (2:2). Christ's glory includes his resurrection, exaltation, and second coming.

2:2 *your meeting* (literally *your synagogue*): This word refers to the gathering of people rather than the building in which they met. • The *fancy clothes and expensive jewelry* of the rich, in contrast to the *dirty clothes* of the poor, symbolize the contrast in socioeconomic status.

2:3-4 It is natural to *give special attention* to wealthy people because of their social status, political power, and potential generosity as patrons. By serving and publicly honoring the wealthy, the church could gain whatever

economic benefits they wished to give. James warns that *this discrimination* reflects *evil motives,* a division between loyalty to God (1:6) and a desire for the benefits of worldly wealth (4:4).

2:5 *Listen to me:* Employing this rhetorical device for emphasis (see Deut 6:3; Amos 3:1; Matt 13:18; Acts 15:13), James presents his argument against favoring the rich. • *Hasn't God chosen the poor?* God's special concern for the poor is reflected in the OT (Exod 23:11; 1 Sam 2:8; Ps 12:5) and in the ministries of Jesus and Paul (Luke 4:18; 6:20; 1 Cor 1:26-28). This concern was emphasized by the Jerusalem church (Gal 2:9-10), of which James was the leader. • *inherit the Kingdom:* The Kingdom of God was central to the teaching of Jesus (Matt 12:8; Mark 1:15; Luke 17:21). Christ already rules from his place at the right hand of the Father, yet his Kingdom will be fully realized only when the Son of Man comes (Matt 25:31, 34; 1 Cor 15:24-28).

2:7 *slander Jesus Christ, whose noble name you bear* (literally *slander the noble name spoken over you*): The name *spoken over you* is Jesus Christ (2:1). It is a sign of ownership, pronounced at the time of conversion and baptism.

2:8-13 James applies biblical evidence to counter the common practice of favoring rich and powerful people.

2:8 Christians are to *obey* (literally *fulfill*) *the royal law,* just as Jesus fulfilled the law by his coming (Matt 5:17) and his teaching (Matt 22:34-40). • The law is

2:10
Matt 5:19
ᵏ*nomos* (3551)
▸ Jas 4:11

2:11
*Exod 20:13-14
*Deut 5:17-18

2:12
ᵃ*eleutheria* (1657)
▸ 1 Pet 2:16

2:13
Matt 18:32-35
Luke 6:38
ᵇ*eleos* (1656)
▸ Jas 3:17

2:14
ᶜ*pistis* (4102)
▸ Jas 2:20

2:16
1 Jn 3:17-18

2:18
Matt 7:16-17

2:19
ᵈ*daimonion* (1140)
▸ Rev 16:14

2:20
ᵉ*pistis* (4102)
▸ 1 Jn 3:23

2:21
Gen 22:9, 12

2:22
Heb 11:17

your neighbor as yourself." ⁹But if you favor some people over others, you are committing a sin. You are guilty of breaking the law. ¹⁰For the person who keeps all of the ᵏlaws except one is as guilty as a person who has broken all of God's laws. ¹¹For the same God who said, "You must not commit adultery," also said, "You must not murder." So if you murder someone but do not commit adultery, you have still broken the law. ¹²So whatever you say or whatever you do, remember that you will be judged by the law that sets you ᵃfree. ¹³There will be no mercy for those who have not shown ᵇmercy to others. But if you have been merciful, God will be ᵇmerciful when he judges you.

Faith without Good Deeds Is Dead

¹⁴What good is it, dear brothers and sisters, if you say you have ᶜfaith but don't show it by your actions? Can that kind of ᶜfaith save anyone? ¹⁵Suppose you see a brother or sister who has no food or clothing, ¹⁶and you say, "Good-bye and have a good day; stay warm and eat well"—but then you don't give that person any food or clothing. What good does that do?

¹⁷So you see, faith by itself isn't enough. Unless it produces good deeds, it is dead and useless.

¹⁸Now someone may argue, "Some people have faith; others have good deeds." But I say, "How can you show me your faith if you don't have good deeds? I will show you my faith by my good deeds."

¹⁹You say you have faith, for you believe that there is one God. Good for you! Even the ᵈdemons believe this, and they tremble in terror. ²⁰How foolish! Can't you see that ᵉfaith without good deeds is useless?

²¹Don't you remember that our ancestor Abraham was shown to be right with God by his actions when he offered his son Isaac on the altar? ²²You see, his faith and his actions worked together. His actions

. . . .

Faith and Faithfulness (2:14-26)

Gen 17:1; 22:1-19
Lev 22:31
1 Sam 2:9
Hab 2:4
John 15:2
Rom 2:6
Gal 5:6; 6:5-10
Eph 2:8-10
Phil 2:12-13
Heb 11:1-40

James's conspicuous emphasis on faithfulness to God argues for charitable deeds as an expression of faith (2:14-26). A faith relationship with God cannot be based merely on believing a true statement (2:19). Saving faith (2:14) results in actions (1:22-25) which emulate God, who generously gives good gifts (1:5, 17; 4:6). Faith and good deeds are inseparable. As with Abraham, good deeds show that a person has complete faith (1:4) and is righteous before God (2:23; Gen 15:6).

Our Lord taught (Matt 5:16) and modeled faith that does good deeds, and Paul also affirmed the need for good deeds (Rom 2:6; Gal 6:5-10; Eph 2:10; Phil 2:12-13; 1 Thes 1:3). Christians are to endure testings (1:3) and temptations (1:13-14), receive wisdom (1:5-6), inherit the Kingdom (2:5), pray for the sick, receive forgiveness (5:15), and rescue the wanderer (5:20). All of these things can be understood as "faith expressing itself in love" (Gal 5:6).

. . . .

called *royal* because it belongs to the Kingdom (2:5) and was articulated by our glorious Lord (King). • *as found in the Scriptures:* James changes from a general reference to the law to a specific written commandment from the holiness code (Lev 19:1-37). It specifies how our love for God is to be expressed in relationships with other people (see Deut 6:5; Lev 19:18). • *"Love your neighbor as yourself":* This quotation from Lev 19:18 requires identifying with the neighbor as though the neighbor were yourself.

2:9 Favoritism violates the command to love one's neighbor (2:8).

2:11 This verse quotes Exod 20:13-14; Deut 5:17-18.

2:12 *The law . . . sets you free* from the controlling power of sin (see 1:25 and note) and thereby promotes endurance and growth toward perfection (1:3-4).

2:13 James concludes this section (2:1-13) by correlating divine mercy with human mercy (see also Matt 6:14-15; Eph 4:32).

2:14-26 James explains why Christians need to be concerned about the judgment of their actions (2:12-13): Real faith must be accompanied by good deeds (see 1:22-25).

2:14 *if you say you have faith:* James writes to Christians who need to be stimulated to produce *actions* that should arise from genuine faith. Paul makes the same point (see, e.g., Gal 5:6) but often criticizes people for trying to base their relationship with God on what they do (Rom 3:20, 28; 4:3-5; Gal 2:16; 3:1-14).

2:15-16 *Suppose you see:* As in 2:2-4, James gives an illustration of "faith" that is useless. • *no food or clothing:* In first-century Palestine and the Roman world in general, many poverty-stricken persons lacked the bare necessities of life. • *stay warm and eat well:* This sentence probably expresses a presumption that God would provide the needs of the poor person. The speaker might suppose that he needs only to express his faith to make it happen. But without his participation (action), it is an empty wish.

2:18-19 James demonstrates the futility of believing that something is true without acting upon it. • *Now someone may argue:* James presents another diatribe (see note on 1:13), in which he presents a hypothetical counter-argument that one person may have the gift of faith while another person has the gift of works (see 1 Cor 12:7-9).

2:19 *that there is one God:* Some manuscripts read *that God is one;* see Deut 6:4, which is the basic confession of Israel's faith. • *the demons believe:* They know that there is one God, and he is their enemy (Mark 1:24).

2:20-26 James demonstrates from Scripture that genuine faith finds expression in action.

2:22 This verse explains 2:21 so it won't be misunderstood: Abraham was not justified by *his actions* alone; instead, *his faith and his actions worked together.* This describes the full scope of Abraham's faithful response to God throughout his life (see Gen 12:1-4; 18:1-27).

made his faith complete. 23And so it happened just as the Scriptures say: "Abraham believed God, and God counted him as righteous because of his faith." He was even called the friend of God. 24So you see, we are shown to be right with God by what we do, not by faith alone.

25Rahab the prostitute is another example. She was shown to be right with God by her actions when she hid those messengers and sent them safely away by a different road. 26Just as the body is dead without breath, so also faith is dead without good works.

5. SPEECH AND CONFLICT (3:1–4:3)
Controlling the Tongue

3 Dear brothers and sisters, not many of you should become teachers in the church, for we who teach will be judged more strictly. 2Indeed, we all make many mistakes. For if we could control our tongues, we would be fperfect and could also control ourselves in every other way.

3We can make a large horse go wherever we want by means of a small bit in its mouth. 4And a small rudder makes a huge ship turn wherever the pilot chooses to go, even though the winds are strong. 5In the same way, the tongue is a small thing that makes grand speeches.

But a tiny spark can set a great forest on fire. 6And the tongue is a flame of fire. It is a whole world of wickedness, corrupting your entire body. It can set your whole life on fire, for it is set on fire by ghell itself.

7People can tame all kinds of animals, birds, reptiles, and fish, 8but no one can tame the htongue. It is restless and evil, full of deadly poison. 9Sometimes it praises our Lord and Father, and sometimes it curses those who have been made in the image of God. 10And so iblessing and cursing come pouring out of the same mouth. Surely, my brothers and sisters, this is not right! 11Does a spring of water bubble out with both fresh water and bitter water? 12Does a fig tree produce olives, or a jgrapevine produce figs? No, and you can't draw fresh water from a salty spring.

True Wisdom Comes from God
13If you are wise and understand God's ways, prove it by living an honorable life, doing good works with the humility that comes from wisdom. 14But if you are bitterly jealous and there is selfish ambition in your heart, don't cover up the truth with boasting

2:23
*Gen 15:6
Isa 41:8
Rom 4:3-5

2:25
Josh 2:4, 6, 15
Heb 11:31

3:1
Luke 12:48
Rom 2:21

3:2
fteleios (5046)
▸ Matt 5:48

3:3
Ps 32:9

3:5
Prov 26:20

3:6
Prov 16:27
Matt 12:36-37; 15:11, 18-19
ggeenna (1067)
▸ Rev 1:18

3:8
Ps 140:3
Rom 3:13
hglōssa (1100)
▸ Mark 16:17

3:9
Gen 1:26-27; 5:1
1 Cor 11:7

3:10
ieulogia (2129)
▸ 1 Pet 3:9

3:12
Matt 7:16
jampelos (0288)
▸ Matt 26:29

3:14
2 Cor 12:20

2:23 *it happened just as the Scriptures say* (literally *the Scripture was fulfilled*): James saw the offering of Isaac (Gen 22) as the fulfillment of Abraham's pledge of faith and God's declaration of Abraham's righteousness (quoted from Gen 15:6). • *He was even called the friend of God:* See Isa 41:8. James emphasizes the nature of faith as a relationship of undivided loyalty (1:5-8; 4:4; John 15:15).

2:24 *not by faith alone:* That is, not like the demons who merely believe something is true (2:19), but by a belief that results in generous deeds like those of God himself (1:17). Though some have thought that this teaching contradicts what Paul taught, it does not. Paul does not speak against good deeds themselves, but about trying to receive forgiveness of sins because of good deeds (Rom 3:28; Gal 2:16). Just as Paul understands that love and generosity necessarily issue from a true faith (Gal 5:6), so also James knows that good deeds can result only from authentic faith that results in a commitment to God (2:18, 26).

2:25 James presents *Rahab the prostitute* (see Josh 2:1) as his second example of good works that must accompany genuine faith. She declared her belief that the Lord God of Israel was the only God (Josh 2:9-11), and her faith was made perfect *by her actions* when she provided hospitality and a

means of escape to the Israelite spies (Josh 2:1-6; 6:25; Heb 11:31).

2:26 *Good works* are as necessary to *faith* as *breath* is to a physical *body* (Gen 2:7). We cannot have one without the other. • *without breath:* Or *without spirit.*

3:1 *Dear brothers and sisters:* Literally *My brothers;* also in 3:10. See note on 2:1. • Becoming *teachers* was one way to improve social status in the early church (1 Cor 12:28; Eph 4:11; 1 Tim 5:17; cp. Acts 5:34). Such honor would compensate for the shame imposed upon Christians as social outsiders (2:6-7). But the conspicuous role of teachers symbolizes the power of human speech to benefit or harm the church.

3:2 *we all:* James's primary concern is with the speech of church members as they influence interpersonal relationships (3:9-10, 14; 4:1-3).

3:6 *It is a whole world of wickedness:* The tongue acts as an agent of the whole unrighteous world which is opposed to God (1:27; 4:4). • *for it is set on fire by hell itself:* Or *for it will burn in hell* (Greek *Gehenna*). *Gehenna* is the place of eternal punishment (Matt 5:22, 30; 23:15), in contrast to *Hades,* the abode of the dead (Luke 16:23; Acts 2:31). The reference to *hell* is an allusion to the devil (4:7; Matt 5:22; John 8:44) as the ultimate source of evil speech.

3:8 *no one can tame the tongue:* The

tongue has an astonishing capacity for committing evil. If its evil is motivated by hell (3:6), it certainly cannot be tamed by mere human effort. • *full of deadly poison:* This might allude to the serpent in the Garden of Eden (Gen 3:1), who is identified with the devil (Rev 20:2).

3:9 *praises . . . curses:* Praising *our Lord and Father* is the best activity of the tongue, whereas cursing *those* made in his *image* is one of the worst, because it is an implicit curse on God himself (Gen 1:26-27; 9:6).

3:11 Some springs, especially in the upper sources of the Jordan River, did produce *fresh water and bitter water;* such brackish springs could not support a town. Similarly, if a person's speech mixes foul with sweet, it will not build up the community.

3:12 *from a salty spring:* Literally *from salt.*

3:13 *If you are wise and understand:* The wisdom that comes from God (1:5) is not mere intellectual skill nor the collection of information, it is practical insight and spiritual understanding which expresses itself in moral uprightness, as described in 3:17-18 (see also Job 28:28; Prov 1:2-4; 2:10-15).

3:14 The *truth* is that wisdom cannot be associated with jealousy and *selfish ambition.* Only in humility can we receive God's true word (1:18, 21).

3:16
1 Cor 3:3
Gal 5:20-21

3:17
Luke 6:36
Rom 12:9
ᵏ*eleos* (1656)
▸ Matt 9:13

3:18
Prov 11:18
Isa 32:17
Matt 5:9
Phil 1:11

4:2
1 Jn 3:15

4:3
1 Jn 3:22; 5:14

4:4
John 15:19
1 Jn 2:15

4:5
1 Cor 6:19
2 Cor 6:16

4:6
*Prov 3:34
Matt 23:12
1 Pet 5:5

4:7
Eph 6:12
1 Pet 5:6-9
ᵃ*diabolos* (1228)
▸ 1 Pet 5:8

4:8
Isa 1:16
Zech 1:3
Mal 3:7

4:9
Luke 6:25

4:10
1 Pet 5:6

4:11
Matt 7:1-5
ᵇ*nomos* (3551)
▸ Matt 7:12

and lying. ¹⁵For jealousy and selfishness are not God's kind of wisdom. Such things are earthly, unspiritual, and demonic. ¹⁶For wherever there is jealousy and selfish ambition, there you will find disorder and evil of every kind.

¹⁷But the wisdom from above is first of all pure. It is also peace loving, gentle at all times, and willing to yield to others. It is full of ᵏmercy and good deeds. It shows no favoritism and is always sincere. ¹⁸And those who are peacemakers will plant seeds of peace and reap a harvest of righteousness.

Conflict from Selfish Prayer

4 What is causing the quarrels and fights among you? Don't they come from the evil desires at war within you? ²You want what you don't have, so you scheme and kill to get it. You are jealous of what others have, but you can't get it, so you fight and wage war to take it away from them. Yet you don't have what you want because you don't ask God for it. ³And even when you ask, you don't get it because your motives are all wrong—you want only what will give you pleasure.

6. DRAWING CLOSE TO GOD (4:4-10)
Seek God's Favor

⁴You adulterers! Don't you realize that friendship with the world makes you an enemy of God? I say it again: If you want to be a friend of the world, you make yourself an enemy of God. ⁵What do you think the Scriptures mean when they say that the spirit God has placed within us is filled with envy? ⁶But he gives us even more grace to stand against such evil desires. As the Scriptures say,

"God opposes the proud
but favors the humble."

Resist the Devil

⁷So humble yourselves before God. Resist the ᵃdevil, and he will flee from you. ⁸Come close to God, and God will come close to you. Wash your hands, you sinners; purify your hearts, for your loyalty is divided between God and the world. ⁹Let there be tears for what you have done. Let there be sorrow and deep grief. Let there be sadness instead of laughter, and gloom instead of joy. ¹⁰Humble yourselves before the Lord, and he will lift you up in honor.

7. WARNINGS (4:11–5:6)
Warning against Judging Others

¹¹Don't speak evil against each other, dear brothers and sisters. If you criticize and judge each other, then you are criticizing and judging God's ᵇlaw. But your job is to obey the ᵇlaw, not to judge whether ᵇit

. . . .

3:15 The wisdom that is *earthly* is not part of the good creation; it is the opposite of heavenly wisdom because it excludes God. It is *unspiritual* because it does not acknowledge or respond to God's Spirit (1 Cor 2:14; Jude 1:19). It is *demonic* since it comes from the devil, the ultimate source of this destructive wisdom (3:6; 4:6; 1 Tim 4:1).

3:18 James uses an agricultural image to emphasize the benefits of living by the wisdom from above: Those who plant *seeds of peace* in relationships will enjoy a luxuriant *harvest of righteousness* (or *of good things, or of justice*) in those relationships (cp. Matt 5:9).

4:1 *quarrels and fights* (literally *wars and battles*): James uses military imagery to declare that their own *evil desires at war within* them were the immediate cause of the battles among church members. James uses the Greek word translated *evil desires* again in 4:3 (translated "pleasure") to enclose the entire paragraph and indicate the source of conflict and unanswered prayer (Luke 8:14; Titus 3:3).

4:2 *you scheme and kill:* Killing was the extreme, but logical, outcome of their rapacious attitude. Some of James's readers might have followed the Jewish Zealot movement and engaged in murder to benefit their cause. Hostile attitudes and violent methods do not provide satisfaction—*you can't get* what you want by them.

4:4-10 James explains the causes of conflict: love for the world, divided loyalty, and arrogant criticism (4:11-12). He gives exhortations which will rectify these causes and lead to peace.

4:4 *You adulterers* (literally *You adulteresses*): James uses this prophetic imagery (see, e.g., Jer 3:6; Hos 3:1) because his readers were seeking what *friendship with the world* could give them—social acceptance (2:1-4), prestige (3:1), or wealth (4:13). Divided loyalty toward God (4:8) is like adultery against one's spouse. • In the ancient world, *friend* was used as a title for special and exclusive relationships (Luke 23:12, Herod and Pilate; John 19:12, Pilate as "friend of Caesar"; see also *1 Maccabees* 2:18; 6:28). Both Moses (Exod 33:11) and Abraham were called friends of God (2:23; 2 Chr 20:7; Isa 41:8; cp. John 15:15). • The *world* consists of society that is opposed to *God* and his kingdom. The world is guided by earthly wisdom, not heavenly (3:15-17), and is characterized by evil desires, fighting, and killing (4:2-3).

4:5 *Scriptures . . . say:* James summa-rizes one of the messages of Scripture, *that the spirit God has placed within us is filled with envy* (or *that God longs jealously for the human spirit he has placed within us,* or *that the Holy Spirit, whom God has placed within us, opposes our envy*).

4:6 *"God opposes the proud but favors the humble":* Prov 3:34 (Greek version).

4:7 *Resist the devil:* See also Eph 6:11; 1 Pet 5:8.

4:8 *Come close to God:* This is the language of friendship (2:23) and loyalty (1:6-8). • *Wash your hands . . . purify your hearts:* The language of ceremonial cleansing is applied to the inner purity of one's actions and intentions (cp. Mark 7:1-23).

4:10 To those who *humble* themselves before him, God gives *honor* in place of the shame of their persecution and oppression (2:6-7).

4:11-12 These verses reflect on Matt 7:1 and Luke 6:37 (see note on 1:22-23).

4:11 *Don't speak evil against each other:* This exhortation for peace in the Christian community requires that Christians not slander each other. Slandering one's neighbor is the same as slandering *God's law,* because the law prohibits slander and demands love

applies to you. [12]God alone, who gave the law, is the Judge. He alone has the power to save or to destroy. So what right do you have to judge your neighbor?

Warning about Self-Confidence

[13]Look here, you who say, "Today or tomorrow we are going to a certain town and will stay there a year. We will do business there and make a profit." [14]How do you know what your life will be like tomorrow? Your life is like the morning fog—it's here a little while, then it's gone. [15]What you ought to say is, "If the Lord wants us to, we will live and do this or that." [16]Otherwise you are boasting about your own plans, and all such boasting is evil.

[17]Remember, it is sin to know what you ought to do and then not do it.

Warning to the Rich

5 Look here, you rich people: Weep and groan with anguish because of all the terrible troubles ahead of you. [2]Your cwealth is rotting away, and your fine clothes are moth-eaten rags. [3]Your gold and silver have become worthless. The very wealth you were counting on will eat away your flesh like fire. This treasure you have accumulated will stand as evidence against you on the day of judgment. [4]For listen! Hear the cries of the field workers whom you have cheated of their pay. The wages you held back cry out against you. The cries of those who harvest your fields have reached the ears of the Lord of Heaven's Armies.

[5]You have spent your years on earth in luxury, satisfying your every desire. You have fattened yourselves for the day of slaughter. [6]You have condemned and killed innocent people, who do not resist you.

8. FINAL EXHORTATIONS (5:7-20)

Patience and Endurance

[7]Dear brothers and sisters, be patient as you wait for the Lord's dreturn. Consider the farmers who patiently wait for the rains in the fall and in the spring. They eagerly look for the valuable harvest to ripen. [8]You, too, must be patient. Take courage, for the coming of the Lord is near.

[9]Don't grumble about each other, brothers and sisters, or you will be judged. For look—the Judge is standing at the door! [10]For examples of patience in suffering, dear brothers and sisters, look at the prophets who spoke in the name of the Lord. [11]We give great honor to those who endure under suffering. For instance, you know about Job, a man of great endurance. You can see how the Lord was kind to him at the end, for the Lord is full of tenderness and mercy.

[12]But most of all, my brothers and sisters, never take an oath, by heaven or earth or

4:12
Rom 2:1; 14:4
4:13-14
Prov 27:1
Luke 12:18-20
4:15
Acts 18:21
4:17
Luke 12:47
5:1
Prov 11:4, 28
5:2
Matt 6:19
^c*ploutos* (4149)
▸ Mark 4:19
5:3
Matt 27:3-5
5:4
Lev 19:13
Deut 24:14-15
Ps 18:6
Luke 12:15-21
5:5
Jer 12:3; 25:34
Luke 16:19-23
5:7
Deut 11:14
Jer 5:24
Joel 2:23
^d*parousia* (3952)
▸ 2 Pet 3:4
5:8
Rom 13:11-12
Heb 10:37
5:9
Matt 24:33
1 Cor 4:5
5:10
Matt 5:12
5:11
Job 1:20-22; 2:7-10;
42:10-17
Ps 103:8
5:12
Matt 5:34-37

. . . .

for one's neighbor (2:8; Lev 19:16-18; Matt 7:1-5). • *dear brothers and sisters:* Literally *brothers;* see note on 2:1.

4:13-16 Itinerant merchants depended on personal assertiveness as a solution to their poverty and low social status. James urges greater recognition of God's providence and warns against arrogantly planning events which one cannot really control.

4:15 The *Lord* has authority over life and death (Deut 32:39; 1 Sam 2:6; Matt 10:28).

4:16 Christians may boast about what God has done (1:9-10), but not about their own arrogant *plans,* which assume that God has no claim or authority over their lives.

4:17 *Remember:* This verse is probably a maxim that James expected his readers to recognize. Its source is unknown, but it is consistent with the teaching of Scripture (cp. Deut 24:15; Prov 3:27-28; Matt 25:41-46; Luke 12:47).

5:1-6 This section denounces the *rich people* for their greed and arrogant oppression of the poor (Lev 19:13). James warns them to repent while they can; if they do not, they will face *terrible troubles . . . on the day of judgment.*

5:2 The *wealth* and *fine clothes* are so excessive that they deteriorate from lack of use; their destruction is a sign of the anticipated judgment.

5:3 Material wealth, represented by *gold* and *silver,* is *worthless* in the face of God's *judgment.* In fact, it *will stand as evidence against* them because it was unjustly gotten (5:4) and wickedly used (5:5-6).

5:4 These rich people (5:1) were exploitive landowners. Like those in 2:6 who oppressed and dragged Christians into court, they were exploiting the day laborers whose work was to *harvest* their *fields.* • *cries . . . have reached the ears of the Lord:* God hears the prayers of the oppressed (see Deut 24:14-15). Even while the laborers are still suffering, the Lord has heard (see Exod 3:7). • *the Lord of Heaven's Armies* (1 Sam 17:45; Ps 103:20-21; Rom 9:29): This title emphasizes God's power to act when the oppressed cannot.

5:6 *killed innocent people* (or *killed the Righteous One*): In this context, the phrase most likely refers to innocent people such as the oppressed laborers in this paragraph rather than to Jesus

(cp. Acts 3:14; 7:52). • *who do not resist you:* Or *Don't they resist you?* or *God oppose you?* or *Aren't they now accusing you before God?*

5:7-8 *Dear brothers and sisters:* Literally *Brothers;* also in 5:9, 10, 12, 19. See note on 2:1. • *be patient:* This is the ultimate resolution for the poor in their economic pressures and for the unjust treatment by the wicked rich (5:1-6; see 2:6-7). Even though the poor have been marginalized and oppressed, they must not give up nor strike out at their oppressors. At *the Lord's return,* the faithful will receive their final reward (Isa 40:10; Luke 6:20-35; 1 Cor 15:23; 1 Pet 1:17; 5:4; Rev 22:12).

5:9 *the Judge is standing at the door!* The coming of Christ is imminent.

5:10 This verse reflects on Matt 5:11 and Luke 6:23 (see note on 1:22-23).

5:11 *Job* was *a man of great endurance* because he remained faithful to God throughout his hardships (Job 1:20-21; 2:9-10) despite his complaints (Job 3:1-26; 12:1-3; 16:1-3).

5:12 *never take an oath:* Because the churches were having such severe verbal conflicts (4:1-3, 11-12), James calls upon them to avoid the pitfalls of

5:13
Col 3:16

5:14
aleiphō (0218)
‣ Matt 6:17

5:15
hamartia (0266)
‣ 1 Jn 1:9

5:16
Matt 18:15-18
1 Jn 1:9

5:17
1 Kgs 17:1-7
Luke 4:25

5:18
1 Kgs 18:42-45

5:19
Matt 18:15

5:20
Prov 10:12
1 Pet 4:8

anything else. Just say a simple yes or no, so that you will not sin and be condemned.

The Power of Prayer

13Are any of you suffering hardships? You should pray. Are any of you happy? You should sing praises. 14Are any of you sick? You should call for the elders of the church to come and pray over you, eanointing you with oil in the name of the Lord. 15Such a prayer offered in faith will heal the sick, and the Lord will make you well. And if you have committed any fsins, you will be forgiven.

16Confess your sins to each other and pray for each other so that you may be healed. The earnest prayer of a righteous person has great power and produces wonderful results. 17Elijah was as human as we are, and yet when he prayed earnestly that no rain would fall, none fell for three and a half years! 18Then, when he prayed again, the sky sent down rain and the earth began to yield its crops.

Restore Wandering Believers

19My dear brothers and sisters, if someone among you wanders away from the truth and is brought back, 20you can be sure that whoever brings the sinner back will save that person from death and bring about the forgiveness of many sins.

The Future Coming of the Lord (5:7-9)

1 Sam 2:10
Ps 2:7-12; 96:11-13
Isa 26:21
Mic 1:3
Matt 16:27
Luke 12:35-48; 18:8
John 5:22-30
Acts 10:42
1 Cor 4:5
1 Jn 2:28

James announces the future coming of the Lord as Judge (5:7-9; cp. Isa 26:21; Mic 1:3). There will be a day of judgment (5:3). God, who gave the law, is the Judge who has the power to save and destroy (4:12). Those who oppress Christians and slander Jesus Christ (2:6-7) will be slaughtered (5:5-6). Those who follow Christ will be judged by the law that was intended to set them free (2:12) if they neglect to show mercy (2:13), befriend the world (4:4), sin through speech and strife (4:11; 5:9), or live to satisfy evil desires (4:1, 16).

The Lord's coming influences present realities. God already honors the faithful poor and humiliates the exploitative rich (1:9-10; 5:2-3). Christians have already become God's prized possession as God is restoring all things (1:18). James declares that we should obey the royal law of the messianic kingdom (2:8), to which Christians have become heirs (2:5).

The coming of the Lord may not be immediate, so James exhorts Christians to endure (1:4) and wait patiently for Christ's return (5:7-8). Christians will receive the crown of eternal life (1:12) and reap the harvest of righteousness sown by a life of faithfulness to God (3:18).

In view of impending judgment, James exhorts Christians to resist the devil and to humble themselves before God (4:7). We must grieve over sin, live with pure intentions and behavior (4:8-9), and rescue any Christian brother or sister who is headed toward death (5:19-20). Like Elijah, we must practice faith, prayer, and confession (5:13-17). Like Job, we must endure suffering to learn how kind the Lord is at the end (4:10; 5:11).

deceitful oaths by not using any oaths at all (Matt 5:33-37). To swear an oath in the name of the Lord was to call upon him to enforce the oath (Gen 31:53; 1 Kgs 8:31-32). When people swore *by heaven or earth* they were either feigning reverence while avoiding the use of the divine name, or they were being deceitful with clever verbiage (see Matt 23:16-22). Peter used an oath deceitfully (Matt 26:71-73), but Paul used an oath to confirm his assertions (Rom 1:9; 2 Cor 1:23), which suggests that the prohibition of oaths is not absolute.

5:14 *The elders of the church* were responsible for the well-being of a local assembly of Christians. Elders were selected because of their relative age and their qualifications as Christian leaders (Acts 14:23; 20:17, 28; 1 Pet 5:1-4; cp. 1 Tim 3:1-7; Titus 1:5-9). • At this

early stage in the development of the church (AD 40s; see James Introduction, "Date and Location of Writing," p. 2111), the word *church* is apparently a non-technical term meaning "congregation, assembly" (cp. Matt 18:17). • The act of *anointing . . . with oil* symbolizes divine blessing and healing (Isa 1:6; Matt 6:17; Mark 6:13; Luke 10:34).

5:15 *a prayer offered in faith will heal the sick:* This proverb is a generally true statement, subject to the will of God. Only prayers that embody true *faith* will be answered affirmatively by the Lord, and faith for a particular healing is a gift that comes from God. See also Mark 9:23; John 14:13-14; 15:7, 16; 16:23-27; 1 Jn 3:22; 5:14-15. • *if you have committed any sins:* James suggests that some illnesses might be caused by sin, and it is important that the sin also be

confessed and *forgiven* (5:16; see Mark 2:3-12; John 5:14).

5:17 *Elijah . . . prayed:* See 1 Kgs 17:1; 18:41-46. • *three and a half years* (see 1 Kgs 18:1; Luke 4:25) is a round figure, half of seven, which symbolizes a period of judgment (cp. Dan 12:7; Rev 11:2).

5:19-20 These verses end the letter as a bookend (*inclusio*) counterbalancing the exhortation to endurance in 1:2-4.

5:20 To *save* a sinner *from death* refers not merely to physical death but to eternal death, the punishment of departing from the truth of the Good News of Jesus Christ (see 1:12, 15; cp. Heb 6:4-8). If the sinful person listens and repents, eternal punishment will be averted (see also Gal 6:1; Jude 1:22-24).

INTRODUCTION TO THE
NEW LIVING TRANSLATION

*Translation Philosophy
and Methodology*
English Bible translations tend to
be governed by one of two general
translation theories. The first
theory has been called "formal-
equivalence," "literal," or "word-for-
word" translation. According to this
theory, the translator attempts to
render each word of the original
language into English and seeks
to preserve the original syntax
and sentence structure as much
as possible in translation. The
second theory has been called
"dynamic-equivalence," "functional-
equivalence," or "thought-for-
thought" translation. The goal of
this translation theory is to produce
in English the closest natural equivalent of the message expressed by
the original-language text, both in
meaning and in style.

Both of these translation theories have their strengths. A formal-
equivalence translation preserves
aspects of the original text—
including ancient idioms, term
consistency, and original-language
syntax—that are valuable for scholars and professional study. It
allows a reader to trace formal elements of the original-language text
through the English translation. A
dynamic-equivalence translation,
on the other hand, focuses on
translating the message of the
original-language text. It ensures
that the meaning of the text is
readily apparent to the contemporary reader. This allows the message
to come through with immediacy,
without requiring the reader to
struggle with foreign idioms and
awkward syntax. It also facilitates
serious study of the text's message
and clarity in both devotional and
public reading.

The pure application of either
of these translation philosophies
would create translations at opposite ends of the translation spectrum. But in reality, all translations
contain a mixture of these two
philosophies. A purely formal-
equivalence translation would
be unintelligible in English, and
a purely dynamic-equivalence
translation would risk being
unfaithful to the original. That
is why translations shaped by
dynamic-equivalence theory are
usually quite literal when the original text is relatively clear, and the
translations shaped by formal-
equivalence theory are sometimes
quite dynamic when the original
text is obscure.

The translators of the New
Living Translation set out to render the message of the original
texts of Scripture into clear, contemporary English. As they did so,
they kept the concerns of both
formal-equivalence and dynamic-
equivalence in mind. On the one
hand, they translated as simply
and literally as possible when that
approach yielded an accurate, clear,
and natural English text. Many
words and phrases were rendered
literally and consistently into
English, preserving essential literary and rhetorical devices, ancient
metaphors, and word choices that
give structure to the text and provide echoes of meaning from one
passage to the next.

On the other hand, the translators rendered the message more
dynamically when the literal rendering was hard to understand, was
misleading, or yielded archaic or
foreign wording. They clarified difficult metaphors and terms to aid
in the reader's understanding. The
translators first struggled with the
meaning of the words and phrases
in the ancient context; then they
rendered the message into clear,
natural English. Their goal was to
be both faithful to the ancient texts

and eminently readable. The result
is a translation that is both exegeti-
cally accurate and idiomatically
powerful.

Translation Process and Team
To produce an accurate translation
of the Bible into contemporary
English, the translation team needed the skills necessary to enter into
the thought patterns of the ancient
authors and then to render their
ideas, connotations, and effects
into clear, contemporary English.
To begin this process, qualified
biblical scholars were needed to
interpret the meaning of the original text and to check it against our
base English translation. In order
to guard against personal and theological biases, the scholars needed
to represent a diverse group of
evangelicals who would employ
the best exegetical tools. Then to
work alongside the scholars, skilled
English stylists were needed to
shape the text into clear, contemporary English.

With these concerns in mind,
the Bible Translation Committee
recruited teams of scholars that
represented a broad spectrum of
denominations, theological perspectives, and backgrounds within
the worldwide evangelical community. (These scholars are listed at
the end of this introduction.) Each
book of the Bible was assigned to
three different scholars with prov-
en expertise in the book or group
of books to be reviewed. Each of
these scholars made a thorough
review of a base translation and
submitted suggested revisions to
the appropriate Senior Translator.
The Senior Translator then
reviewed and summarized these
suggestions and proposed a first-
draft revision of the base text. This
draft served as the basis for several
additional phases of exegetical and

stylistic committee review. Then the Bible Translation Committee jointly reviewed and approved every verse of the final translation.

Throughout the translation and editing process, the Senior Translators and their scholar teams were given a chance to review the editing done by the team of stylists. This ensured that exegetical errors would not be introduced late in the process and that the entire Bible Translation Committee was happy with the final result. By choosing a team of qualified scholars and skilled stylists and by setting up a process that allowed their interaction throughout the process, the New Living Translation has been refined to preserve the essential formal elements of the original biblical texts, while also creating a clear, understandable English text.

The New Living Translation was first published in 1996. Shortly after its initial publication, the Bible Translation Committee began a process of further committee review and translation refinement. The purpose of this continued revision was to increase the level of precision without sacrificing the text's easy-to-understand quality. This second-edition text was completed in 2004, and an additional update with minor changes was subsequently introduced in 2007. This printing of the New Living Translation reflects the updated 2007 text.

Written to Be Read Aloud
It is evident in Scripture that the biblical documents were written to be read aloud, often in public worship (see Nehemiah 8; Luke 4:16-20; 1 Timothy 4:13; Revelation 1:3). It is still the case today that more people will hear the Bible read aloud in church than are likely to read it for themselves. Therefore, a new translation must communicate with clarity and power when it is read publicly. Clarity was a primary goal for the NLT translators, not only to facilitate private reading and understanding, but also to ensure that it would be excellent for public reading and make an immediate and powerful impact on any listener.

The Texts behind the
New Living Translation
The Old Testament translators used the Masoretic Text of the Hebrew

Bible as represented in *Biblia Hebraica Stuttgartensia* (1977), with its extensive system of textual notes; this is an update of Rudolf Kittel's *Biblia Hebraica* (Stuttgart, 1937). The translators also further compared the Dead Sea Scrolls, the Septuagint and other Greek manuscripts, the Samaritan Pentateuch, the Syriac Peshitta, the Latin Vulgate, and any other versions or manuscripts that shed light on the meaning of difficult passages.

The New Testament translators used the two standard editions of the Greek New Testament: the *Greek New Testament,* published by the United Bible Societies (UBS, fourth revised edition, 1993), and *Novum Testamentum Graece,* edited by Nestle and Aland (NA, twenty-seventh edition, 1993). These two editions, which have the same text but differ in punctuation and textual notes, represent, for the most part, the best in modern textual scholarship. However, in cases where strong textual or other scholarly evidence supported the decision, the translators sometimes chose to differ from the UBS and NA Greek texts and followed variant readings found in other ancient witnesses. Significant textual variants of this sort are always noted in the textual notes of the New Living Translation.

Translation Issues
The translators have made a conscious effort to provide a text that can be easily understood by the typical reader of modern English. To this end, we sought to use only vocabulary and language structures in common use today. We avoided using language likely to become quickly dated or that reflects only a narrow subdialect of English, with the goal of making the New Living Translation as broadly useful and timeless as possible.

But our concern for readability goes beyond the concerns of vocabulary and sentence structure. We are also concerned about historical and cultural barriers to understanding the Bible, and we have sought to translate terms shrouded in history and culture in ways that can be immediately understood. To this end:

- We have converted ancient weights and measures (for

example, "ephah" [a unit of dry volume] or "cubit" [a unit of length]) to modern English (American) equivalents, since the ancient measures are not generally meaningful to today's readers. Then in the textual footnotes we offer the literal Hebrew, Aramaic, or Greek measures, along with modern metric equivalents.

- Instead of translating ancient currency values literally, we have expressed them in common terms that communicate the message. For example, in the Old Testament, "ten shekels of silver" becomes "ten pieces of silver" to convey the intended message. In the New Testament, we have often translated the "denarius" as "the normal daily wage" to facilitate understanding. Then a footnote offers: "Greek *a denarius,* the payment for a full day's wage.*" In general, we give a clear English rendering and then state the literal Hebrew, Aramaic, or Greek in a textual footnote.

- Since the names of Hebrew months are unknown to most contemporary readers, and since the Hebrew lunar calendar fluctuates from year to year in relation to the solar calendar used today, we have looked for clear ways to communicate the time of year the Hebrew months (such as Abib) refer to. When an expanded or interpretive rendering is given in the text, a textual note gives the literal rendering. Where it is possible to define a specific ancient date in terms of our modern calendar, we use modern dates in the text. A textual footnote then gives the literal Hebrew date and states the rationale for our rendering. For example, Ezra 6:15 pinpoints the date when the postexilic Temple was completed in Jerusalem: "the third day of the month Adar." This was during the sixth year of King Darius's reign (that is, 515 B.C.). We have translated that date as March 12, with a footnote giving the Hebrew and identifying the year as 515 B.C.

- Since ancient references to the time of day differ from our modern methods of denoting time, we have used renderings that are instantly understandable to the modern reader. Accordingly, we have rendered specific times of day by using approximate equivalents in terms of our common "o'clock" system. On occasion, translations such as "at dawn the next morning" or "as the sun was setting" have been used when the biblical reference is more general.

• When the meaning of a proper name (or a wordplay inherent in a proper name) is relevant to the message of the text, its meaning is often illuminated with a textual footnote. For example, in Exodus 2:10 the text reads: "The princess named him Moses, for she explained, 'I lifted him out of the water.' " The accompanying footnote reads: "*Moses* sounds like a Hebrew term that means 'to lift out.' "

Sometimes, when the actual meaning of a name is clear, that meaning is included in parentheses within the text itself. For example, the text at Genesis 16:11 reads: "You are to name him Ishmael *(which means 'God hears'),* for the LORD has heard your cry of distress." Since the original hearers and readers would have instantly understood the meaning of the name "Ishmael," we have provided modern readers with the same information so they can experience the text in a similar way.

• Many words and phrases carry a great deal of cultural meaning that was obvious to the original readers but needs explanation in our own culture. For example, the phrase "they beat their breasts" (Luke 23:48) in ancient times meant that people were very upset, often in mourning. In our translation we chose to translate this phrase dynamically for clarity: "They went home *in deep sorrow.*" Then we included a footnote with the literal Greek, which reads: "Greek *went home beating their breasts.*" In other similar cases, however, we have sometimes chosen to illuminate the existing literal expression to make it immediately understandable. For example, here we might have expanded the literal Greek phrase to read: "They went home beating their breasts *in sorrow.*" If we had done this,

we would not have included a textual footnote, since the literal Greek clearly appears in translation.

• Metaphorical language is sometimes difficult for contemporary readers to understand, so at times we have chosen to translate or illuminate the meaning of a metaphor. For example, the ancient poet writes, "Your neck is *like* the tower of David" (Song of Songs 4:4). We have rendered it "Your neck is *as beautiful as* the tower of David" to clarify the intended positive meaning of the simile. Another example comes in Ecclesiastes 12:3, which can be literally rendered: "Remember him . . . when the grinding women cease because they are few, and the women who look through the windows see dimly." We have rendered it: "Remember him before your teeth—your few remaining servants—stop grinding; and before your eyes—the women looking through the windows— see dimly." We clarified such metaphors only when we believed a typical reader might be confused by the literal text.

• When the content of the original language text is poetic in character, we have rendered it in English poetic form. We sought to break lines in ways that clarify and highlight the relationships between phrases of the text. Hebrew poetry often uses parallelism, a literary form where a second phrase (or in some instances a third or fourth) echoes the initial phrase in some way. In Hebrew parallelism, the subsequent parallel phrases continue, while also furthering and sharpening, the thought expressed in the initial line or phrase. Whenever possible, we sought to represent these parallel phrases in natural poetic English.

• The Greek term *hoi Ioudaioi* is literally translated "the Jews" in many English translations. In the Gospel of John, however, this term doesn't always refer to the Jewish people generally. In some contexts, it refers more particularly to the Jewish religious leaders. We have attempted to capture the meaning in these different contexts by using terms such as "the people" (with a

footnote: Greek *the Jewish people*) or "the religious leaders," where appropriate.

• One challenge we faced was how to translate accurately the ancient biblical text that was originally written in a context where male-oriented terms were used to refer to humanity generally. We needed to respect the nature of the ancient context while also trying to make the translation clear to a modern audience that tends to read male-oriented language as applying only to males. Often the original text, though using masculine nouns and pronouns, clearly intends that the message be applied to both men and women. A typical example is found in the New Testament letters, where the believers are called "brothers" (*adelphoi*). Yet it is clear from the content of these letters that they were addressed to all the believers— male and female. Thus, we have usually translated this Greek word as "brothers and sisters" in order to represent the historical situation more accurately.

We have also been sensitive to passages where the text applies generally to human beings or to the human condition. In some instances we have used plural pronouns (they, them) in place of the masculine singular (he, him). For example, a traditional rendering of Proverbs 22:6 is: "Train up a child in the way he should go, and when he is old he will not turn from it." We have rendered it: "Direct your children onto the right path, and when they are older, they will not leave it." At times, we have also replaced third person pronouns with the second person to ensure clarity. A traditional rendering of Proverbs 26:27 is: "He who digs a pit will fall into it, and he who rolls a stone, it will come back on him." We have rendered it: "If you set a trap for others, you will get caught in it yourself. If you roll a boulder down on others, it will crush you instead."

We should emphasize, however, that all masculine nouns and pronouns used to represent God (for example, "Father") have been maintained without exception. All decisions of this kind have been driven by the concern to reflect accurately the intended meaning of the original texts of Scripture.

Lexical Consistency in Terminology
For the sake of clarity, we have translated certain original-language terms consistently, especially within synoptic passages and for commonly repeated rhetorical phrases, and within certain word categories such as divine names and non-theological technical terminology (e.g., liturgical, legal, cultural, zoological, and botanical terms). For theological terms, we have allowed a greater semantic range of acceptable English words or phrases for a single Hebrew or Greek word. We have avoided some theological terms that are not readily understood by many modern readers. For example, we avoided using words such as "justification" and "sanctification," which are carryovers from Latin translations. In place of these words, we have provided renderings such as "made right with God" and "made holy."

The Spelling of Proper Names
Many individuals in the Bible, especially the Old Testament, are known by more than one name (e.g., Uzziah/Azariah). For the sake of clarity, we have tried to use a single spelling for any one individual, footnoting the literal spelling whenever we differ from it. This is especially helpful in delineating the kings of Israel and Judah. King Joash/Jehoash of Israel has been consistently called Jehoash, while King Joash/Jehoash of Judah is called Joash. A similar distinction has been used to distinguish between Joram/Jehoram of Israel and Joram/Jehoram of Judah. All such decisions were made with the goal of clarifying the text for the reader. When the ancient biblical writers clearly had a theological purpose in their choice of a variant name (e.g., Esh-baal/Ishbosheth), the different names have been maintained with an explanatory footnote.

For the names Jacob and Israel, which are used interchangeably for both the individual patriarch and the nation, we generally render it

"Israel" when it refers to the nation and "Jacob" when it refers to the individual. When our rendering of the name differs from the underlying Hebrew text, we provide a textual footnote, which includes this explanation: "The names 'Jacob' and 'Israel' are often interchanged throughout the Old Testament, referring sometimes to the individual patriarch and sometimes to the nation."

The Rendering of Divine Names
All appearances of *'el, 'elohim,* or *'eloah* have been translated "God," except where the context demands the translation "god(s)." We have generally rendered the tetragrammaton (*YHWH*) consistently as "the LORD," utilizing a form with small capitals that is common among English translations. This will distinguish it from the name *'adonai,* which we render "Lord." When *'adonai* and *YHWH* appear together, we have rendered it "Sovereign LORD." This also distinguishes *'adonai YHWH* from cases where *YHWH* appears with *'elohim,* which is rendered "LORD God." When *YH* (the short form of *YHWH*) and *YHWH* appear together, we have rendered it "LORD GOD." When *YHWH* appears with the term *tseba'oth,* we have rendered it "LORD of Heaven's Armies" to translate the meaning of the name. In a few cases, we have utilized the transliteration, *Yahweh,* when the personal character of the name is being invoked in contrast to another divine name or the name of some other god (for example, see Exodus 3:15; 6:2-3).

In the New Testament, the Greek word *christos* has been translated as "Messiah" when the context assumes a Jewish audience. When a Gentile audience can be assumed, *christos* has been translated as "Christ." The Greek word *kurios* is consistently translated "Lord," except that it is translated "LORD" wherever the New Testament text explicitly quotes from the Old Testament, and the text there has it in small capitals.

Textual Footnotes
The New Living Translation provides several kinds of textual footnotes, all included within the study notes in this edition:

- When for the sake of clarity the NLT renders a difficult or potentially confusing phrase dynamically, we generally give the literal rendering in a textual footnote. This allows the reader to see the literal source of our dynamic rendering and how our transation relates to other more literal translations. These notes are prefaced with "literally." For example, in Acts 2:42 we translated the literal "breaking of bread" (from the Greek) as "the Lord's Supper" to clarify that this verse refers to the ceremonial practice of the church rather than just an ordinary meal. Then we attached a footnote to "the Lord's Supper," which reads: "Literally *the breaking of bread.*"

- Textual footnotes are also used to show alternative renderings, prefaced with the word "Or." These normally occur for passages where an aspect of the meaning is debated. On occasion, we also provide notes on words or phrases that represent a departure from long-standing tradition. These notes are prefaced with "Traditionally rendered." For example, the footnote to the translation "serious skin disease" at Leviticus 13:2 says: "Traditionally rendered *leprosy.* The Hebrew word used throughout this passage is used to describe various skin diseases."

- When our translators follow a textual variant that differs significantly from our standard Hebrew or Greek texts (listed earlier), we document that difference with a footnote. We also footnote cases when the NLT excludes a passage that is included in the Greek text known as the *Textus Receptus* (and familiar to readers through its translation in the King James Version). In such cases, we offer a translation of the excluded text in a footnote, even though it is generally recognized as a later addition to the Greek text and not part of the original Greek New Testament.

- All Old Testament passages that are quoted in the New Testament are identified by a textual footnote at the New Testament location. When the New Testament clearly quotes from the Greek translation of the Old Testament, and when it differs significantly in wording from the Hebrew text, we also place a textual footnote at the Old Testament location. This note includes a rendering of the Greek version, along with a cross-reference to the New Testament passage(s) where it is cited (for example, see notes on Proverbs 3:12; Psalms 8:2; 53:3).

- Some textual footnotes provide cultural and historical information on places, things, and people in the Bible that are probably obscure to modern readers. Such notes should aid the reader in understanding the message of the text. For example, in Acts 12:1, "King Herod" is named in this translation as "King Herod Agrippa" and is identified in a footnote as being "the nephew of Herod Antipas and a grandson of Herod the Great."
- When the meaning of a proper name (or a wordplay inherent in a proper name) is relevant to the meaning of the text, it is either illuminated with a textual footnote or included within parentheses in the text itself. For example, the footnote concerning the name "Eve" at Genesis

3:20 reads: "*Eve* sounds like a Hebrew term that means 'to give life.' " This wordplay in the Hebrew illuminates the meaning of the text, which goes on to say that Eve "would be the mother of all who live."

Cross-References
There are a number of different cross-referencing tools that appear in New Living Translation Bibles, and they offer different levels of help in this regard. All straight-text Bibles include the standard set of textual footnotes that include cross-references connecting New Testament texts to their related Old Testament sources. (See more on this above.)

Many NLT Bibles include an additional short cross-reference system that sets key cross-references at the end of paragraphs and then marks the associated verses with a cross symbol. This space-efficient system, while not being obtrusive, offers many important key connections between passages. Larger study editions include a full-column cross-reference system. This system allows space for a more comprehensive listing of cross-references.

As we submit this translation for publication, we recognize that any translation of the Scriptures is subject to limitations and imperfections. Anyone who has attempted to communicate the richness of God's Word into another language will realize it is impossible to make a perfect translation. Recognizing these limitations, we sought God's guidance and wisdom throughout this project. Now we pray that he will accept our efforts and use this translation for the benefit of the church and of all people.

We pray that the New Living Translation will overcome some of the barriers of history, culture, and language that have kept people from reading and understanding God's Word. We hope that readers unfamiliar with the Bible will find the words clear and easy to understand and that readers well versed in the Scriptures will gain a fresh perspective. We pray that readers will gain insight and wisdom for living, but most of all that they will meet the God of the Bible and be forever changed by knowing him.

THE BIBLE TRANSLATION COMMITTEE, *October 2007*

BIBLE TRANSLATION TEAM
Holy Bible, New Living Translation

PENTATEUCH
Daniel I. Block, Senior Translator
Wheaton College

GENESIS
Allen Ross, *Beeson Divinity School, Samford University*
Gordon Wenham, *Trinity Theological College, Bristol*

EXODUS
Robert Bergen, *Hannibal-LaGrange College*
Daniel I. Block, *Wheaton College*
Eugene Carpenter, *Bethel College, Mishawaka, Indiana*

LEVITICUS
David Baker, *Ashland Theological Seminary*
Victor Hamilton, *Asbury College*

Kenneth Mathews, *Beeson Divinity School, Samford University*

NUMBERS
Dale A. Brueggemann, *Assemblies of God Division of Foreign Missions*
R. K. Harrison (deceased), *Wycliffe College*
Paul R. House, *Wheaton College*
Gerald L. Mattingly, *Johnson Bible College*

DEUTERONOMY
J. Gordon McConville, *University of Gloucester*
Eugene H. Merrill, *Dallas Theological Seminary*
John A. Thompson (deceased), *University of Melbourne*

HISTORICAL BOOKS
Barry J. Beitzel, Senior Translator
Trinity Evangelical Divinity School

JOSHUA, JUDGES
Carl E. Armerding, *Schloss Mittersill Study Centre*
Barry J. Beitzel, *Trinity Evangelical Divinity School*
Lawson Stone, *Asbury Theological Seminary*

1 & 2 SAMUEL
Robert Gordon, *Cambridge University*
V. Philips Long, *Regent College*
J. Robert Vannoy, *Biblical Theological Seminary*

1 & 2 KINGS
Bill T. Arnold, *Asbury Theological Seminary*

William H. Barnes, *North Central University*

Frederic W. Bush, *Fuller Theological Seminary*

1 & 2 CHRONICLES
Raymond B. Dillard (deceased), *Westminster Theological Seminary*

David A. Dorsey, *Evangelical School of Theology*

Terry Eves, *Erskine College*

RUTH, EZRA—ESTHER
William C. Williams, *Vanguard University*

H. G. M. Williamson, *Oxford University*

WISDOM BOOKS
Tremper Longman III, Senior Translator
Westmont College

JOB
August Konkel, *Providence Theological Seminary*

Tremper Longman III, *Westmont College*

Al Wolters, *Redeemer College*

PSALMS 1–75
Mark D. Futato, *Reformed Theological Seminary*

Douglas Green, *Westminster Theological Seminary*

Richard Pratt, *Reformed Theological Seminary*

PSALMS 76–150
David M. Howard Jr., *Bethel Theological Seminary*

Raymond C. Ortlund Jr., *Trinity Evangelical Divinity School*

Willem VanGemeren, *Trinity Evangelical Divinity School*

PROVERBS
Ted Hildebrandt, *Gordon College*
Richard Schultz, *Wheaton College*
Raymond C. Van Leeuwen, *Eastern College*

ECCLESIASTES, SONG OF SONGS
Daniel C. Fredericks, *Belhaven College*

David Hubbard (deceased), *Fuller Theological Seminary*

Tremper Longman III, *Westmont College*

PROPHETS
John N. Oswalt, Senior Translator
Wesley Biblical Seminary

ISAIAH
John N. Oswalt, *Wesley Biblical Seminary*

Gary Smith, *Midwestern Baptist Theological Seminary*

John Walton, *Wheaton College*

JEREMIAH, LAMENTATIONS
G. Herbert Livingston, *Asbury Theological Seminary*

Elmer A. Martens, *Mennonite Brethren Biblical Seminary*

EZEKIEL
Daniel I. Block, *Wheaton College*
David H. Engelhard, *Calvin Theological Seminary*

David Thompson, *Asbury Theological Seminary*

DANIEL, HAGGAI—MALACHI
Joyce Baldwin Caine (deceased), *Trinity College, Bristol*

Douglas Gropp, *Catholic University of America*

Roy Hayden, *Oral Roberts School of Theology*

Andrew Hill, *Wheaton College*
Tremper Longman III, *Westmont College*

HOSEA—ZEPHANIAH
Joseph Coleson, *Nazarene Theological Seminary*

Roy Hayden, *Oral Roberts School of Theology*

Andrew Hill, *Wheaton College*
Richard Patterson, *Liberty University*

GOSPELS AND ACTS
Grant R. Osborne, Senior Translator
Trinity Evangelical Divinity School

MATTHEW
Craig Blomberg, *Denver Seminary*
Donald A. Hagner, *Fuller Theological Seminary*

David Turner, *Grand Rapids Baptist Seminary*

MARK
Robert Guelich (deceased), *Fuller Theological Seminary*

George Guthrie, *Union University*
Grant R. Osborne, *Trinity Evangelical Divinity School*

LUKE
Darrell Bock, *Dallas Theological Seminary*

Scot McKnight, *North Park University*
Robert Stein, *The Southern Baptist Theological Seminary*

JOHN
Gary M. Burge, *Wheaton College*
Philip W. Comfort, *Coastal Carolina University*

Marianne Meye Thompson, *Fuller Theological Seminary*

ACTS
D. A. Carson, *Trinity Evangelical Divinity School*

William J. Larkin, *Columbia International University*

Roger Mohrlang, *Whitworth University*

LETTERS AND REVELATION
Norman R. Ericson, Senior Translator
Wheaton College

ROMANS, GALATIANS
Gerald Borchert, *Northern Baptist Theological Seminary*

Douglas J. Moo, *Wheaton College*

Thomas R. Schreiner, *The Southern Baptist Theological Seminary*

1 & 2 CORINTHIANS
Joseph Alexanian, *Trinity International University*

Linda Belleville, *Bethel College, Mishawaka, Indiana*

Douglas A. Oss, *Central Bible College*

Robert Sloan, *Baylor University*

EPHESIANS—PHILEMON
Harold W. Hoehner, *Dallas Theological Seminary*

Moises Silva, *Gordon-Conwell Theological Seminary*

Klyne Snodgrass, *North Park Theological Seminary*

HEBREWS, JAMES, 1 & 2 PETER, JUDE
Peter Davids, *Schloss Mittersill Study Centre*

Norman R. Ericson, *Wheaton College*
William Lane (deceased), *Seattle Pacific University*

J. Ramsey Michaels, *S. W. Missouri State University*

1–3 JOHN, REVELATION
Greg Beale, *Wheaton College*
Robert Mounce, *Whitworth University*

M. Robert Mulholland Jr., *Asbury Theological Seminary*

SPECIAL REVIEWERS
F. F. Bruce (deceased), *University of Manchester*

Kenneth N. Taylor (deceased), *Translator*, The Living Bible

COORDINATING TEAM
Mark D. Taylor, *Director and Chief Stylist*

Ronald A. Beers, *Executive Director and Stylist*

Mark R. Norton, *Managing Editor and O.T. Coordinating Editor*

Philip W. Comfort, *N.T. Coordinating Editor*

Daniel W. Taylor, *Bethel University, Senior Stylist*

N L T S T U D Y B I B L E
CONTRIBUTORS

EDITORS

GENERAL EDITOR
Sean A. Harrison

EXECUTIVE EDITOR
Mark D. Taylor

CONTENT EDITORS
David P. Barrett
G. Patrick LaCosse
Bradley J. Lewis
Henry M. Whitney III
Keith Williams

STYLISTIC EDITOR
Linda Schlafer

COPY EDITORS
Keith Williams, Coordinator
Leanne Roberts, Proofreading
   Coordinator
Paul Adams
Jason Driesbach
Adam Graber
Annette Hayward
Judy Modica
Jonathan Schindler
Caleb Sjogren
Cindy Szponder
Lisa Voth
Matthew Wolf

GENERAL REVIEWERS

GENESIS—DEUTERONOMY
Daniel I. Block

JOSHUA—ESTHER, MAPS
Barry J. Beitzel

JOB—SONG OF SONGS
Tremper Longman III

ISAIAH—MALACHI
John N. Oswalt

MATTHEW—ACTS
Grant R. Osborne

ROMANS—REVELATION
Norman R. Ericson

CONTRIBUTING SCHOLARS

GENESIS
Andrew Schmutzer
Allen P. Ross

EXODUS
John N. Oswalt

LEVITICUS
William C. Williams

NUMBERS
Gerald L. Mattingly

DEUTERONOMY
Eugene H. Merrill

JOSHUA
Joseph Coleson

JUDGES
Carl E. Armerding

RUTH
Joseph Coleson
Sean A. Harrison

1 & 2 SAMUEL
Victor P. Hamilton

1 & 2 KINGS
Richard D. Patterson

1 & 2 CHRONICLES
August Konkel

EZRA, NEHEMIAH, ESTHER
Gary V. Smith

JOB
Dale A. Brueggemann

PSALMS
Willem VanGemeren

PROVERBS
Tremper Longman III

ECCLESIASTES
Sean A. Harrison
Daniel C. Fredericks

SONG OF SONGS
Daniel C. Fredericks
Tremper Longman III

ISAIAH
Willem VanGemeren

JEREMIAH, LAMENTATIONS
G. Herbert Livingston

EZEKIEL
Iain Duguid

DANIEL
Gene Carpenter

HOSEA, JOEL
Owen Dickens

AMOS
William C. Williams

OBADIAH
Carl E. Armerding

JONAH
G. Patrick LaCosse

MICAH
Eugene Carpenter

NAHUM, HABAKKUK, ZEPHANIAH
Richard D. Patterson

HAGGAI, ZECHARIAH, MALACHI
Andrew Hill

MATTHEW
Scot McKnight

MARK
Robert Stein

LUKE
Mark Strauss

JOHN
Gary M. Burge

ACTS
Allison Trites

ROMANS
Douglas J. Moo

1 CORINTHIANS
Roger Mohrlang

2 CORINTHIANS
Ralph P. Martin

GALATIANS
Sean A. Harrison

EPHESIANS, PHILIPPIANS,
PHILEMON
Roger Mohrlang

COLOSSIANS
Douglas J. Moo

1 & 2 THESSALONIANS
Gene L. Green

1 & 2 TIMOTHY, TITUS
Jon Laansma

HEBREWS
George Guthrie

JAMES
Norman R. Ericson

1 & 2 PETER, JUDE
Douglas J. Moo

1–3 JOHN
Philip W. Comfort

REVELATION
Gerald Borchert

OLD TESTAMENT PROFILES
Tremper Longman III

NEW TESTAMENT PROFILES
Roger Mohrlang

ARTICLES
Daniel I. Block
Eugene Carpenter
Philip W. Comfort
Iain Duguid
Sean A. Harrison
Tremper Longman III
Douglas J. Moo
Grant R. Osborne

Richard D. Patterson
Daniel H. Williams
William C. Williams

WORD STUDY SYSTEM
James A. Swanson
Keith Williams

SPECIAL REVIEWER
Kenneth N. Taylor (deceased)

BIBLE PUBLISHING TEAM
PUBLISHER
Douglas R. Knox

ASSOCIATE PUBLISHER
Blaine A. Smith

ACQUISITIONS DIRECTOR
Kevin O'Brien

ACQUISITIONS EDITOR
Kim Johnson

OTHER SERVICES
GRAPHIC DESIGNERS
Timothy R. Botts (Interior)
Julie Chen (Cover)

CARTOGRAPHY
David P. Barrett

ILLUSTRATORS
Hugh Claycombe
Luke Daab
Sean A. Harrison

TYPESETTING
Joel Bartlett (The Livingstone
   Corporation)
Gwen Elliott

PROOFREADING
Peachtree Editorial Services

INDEXING
Karen Schmitt
   (Schmitt Indexing)

Many thanks to all who have had a hand
in the creation of this study Bible,
and most of all to the Lord of heaven and earth,
who gave us his word and Spirit so generously.